UP
GRADE

Also by Paul Mort

Paul Mort Will Save Your Life

UP GRADE

THE NO-BULLSH*T GUIDE TO
LEVELLING UP YOUR LIFE

PAUL MORT

Harper North

HarperNorth
Windmill Green
24 Mount Street
Manchester M2 3NX

A division of
HarperCollins*Publishers*
1 London Bridge Street
London SE1 9GF

www.harpercollins.co.uk

HarperCollins*Publishers*
Macken House, 39/40 Mayor Street Upper
Dublin 1, D01 C9W8, Ireland

First published by HarperCollins*Publishers* Ltd 2025
This updated paperback edition published by HarperCollins*Publishers* Ltd 2026

1 3 5 7 9 10 8 6 4 2

A catalogue record of this book is available from the British Library

HB ISBN 978-0-00-871802-2
PB ISBN 978-0-00-871805-3

Printed and bound in the UK using 100% renewable electricity at CPI Group (UK) Ltd

Unfuckwithable

Definition: when you are truly at peace and in touch with yourself, and nothing anyone says or does bothers you, and no negativity can touch you.

Contents

Introduction

Hi, Mush, welcome to your best future!

This book is for everyone who knows they have the potential to be bigger, better and happier, whether that be as a parent, husband, sibling, friend or boss. It's for all of us who suspect that there is always a blue sky behind the clouds, like when a plane ascends and you pass through stormy weather to brighter skies that were there all along, we just couldn't see them.

Or, if it's 'more of the same shit' you're immediately picturing on hearing the word 'future', if you're low on hope and your rope is fraying, then fear not friend. I'm going to help you sort your head out so you can power-flush your mental U-bend, which if you're feeling negative, is likely blocked with old crap and outdated self-beliefs that are now obsolete and stopping you living what I call, a fully electric life.

This is the magic at the heart of *Upgrade*. It's not something far off and unreachable. It's you, but better. But when I say magic, it's not going to happen with a wave of a wand. It comes from some basic truths, dropping the excuses and putting in the time to focus on what we want, and the secret ingredient – doing what we say we're going to.

It will mean throwing out some old ideas that hold us back. We're going to learn how fucking lazy and often untrue our *automatic* thinking is and how not to trust it, that and the shit it dredges up from our past to generate thoughts to hold us back from moving forward.

I'll teach you to check your emotions to master your life – as that, my friend, is how you Upgrade and become 'unfuckwithable'. That's not to say you become a robot, but instead by understanding where your emotions and opinions of others are coming from, you make yourself freer and lighter to move through your life and smash your goals.

I'll teach you that finding your passion and feeding it makes you a hell of a lot happier than making a load of wedge doing something you don't care about. Back in the mid 20-teens, I pretty much sacrificed my soul in pursuit of money and I ended up feeling as hollow as an empty can of Newkie Brown; see, the cash meant nothing because it was too easily earnt and I was lonely as fuck. This and my deeper issues – which we'll get to later – led me to seek the help of a phone book full of shrinks, snake-oil charlatans, psychotherapists, psychologists and therapists. I was diagnosed as bipolar (you might know it as manic depression) in 2014.

And ADHD. What doesn't kill you makes you wiser, right?

From there to here has been a heck of a trip. I'm now two times UK Mastercoach of the Year, a best-selling Audible author and a regular keynote speaker – but I'm also someone who is honest about how I got here. So what am I rattling on about? There's no fluff with my lessons in life, only can-do candour, and there'll be no moss on you rolling stones as you'll be moving quickly and to where you need to be by the time I've finished with you.

And why am I so sure fast, empowered transformation is possible? I've seen it work in person for so many of the people I've coached but mainly it works because of two simple principles. One is about me, the other is about you.

I won't give advice on anything that I haven't been through myself

Yes, I'll share all of my experiences with brutal honesty but beyond those, if I've not lived it, it's not my place to pretend I have – it's my role to give you the tools to recognise and deal with your own blocks. I'm going to give you the belief, accountability and power to make some changes, and I'm going to make sure we don't tell each other excuses.

I only work with people who want to change

This might sound like I'm turning away readers and clients but it's how my method delivers results. I work with people at their turning point and supercharge their journey. Everyone has a different trigger for why they want to change – whether that's just fine-tuning or a whole life turnaround – once you've found your reason for change, I'll show you how you can make that happen. After all, if we knew how simple it could be, most of us would want to change our life for the better. Because remember, when you level up everyone around you benefits: your family, partner, friends and work colleagues.

Do you want to coast or lurk in the shadows and let the weeds grow around you, or do you want to be a fucking legend, upgrading to your full potential, inspiring and leading the way for the people around you?

My no-nonsense tools and strategies will help you identify, picture and realise the life you've secretly been dreaming of but never believed could happen. We'll learn how to neutralise negative thoughts that are blocking our progress, transforming them into positives. As well as working on subconscious habits, I'll show you that the thoughts you consciously think can immediately change the way you feel, and that the way you regard people is a reflection of how you are feeling in yourself at any given moment. When you feel happier, you feel more empathy and generosity for others, and this is when you feel your natural best, connected to the world around you.

I'll show you how the supposedly scary unknown is actually where you find the real treasure, how to embrace it, and how to stop chasing your own tail, going round in circles, repeating self-destructive patterns again and again. Yes, us upright apes are hardwired for bad news and are constantly looking over our shoulder, that's what's kept us alive at the top of the food chain; but let's face it, it's a bit bloody simplistic. I'm going to show you that happiness is an equally natural state that you have the potential to access at any time, it's a fucking superpower you'll never lose once you've discovered how.

I'll help you pin down your purpose and create your desired vision of the future, setting super-compelling goals as well as giving you a set of tools to measure your progress.

Through daily journalling, you can develop your ability to self-reflect objectively and honestly on what's working and what's not. I'll look at scarcity and our tendency to undersell ourselves, replacing it with a kick-ass abundance mindset, from which money flows easily to you from everywhere.

The tools I'm going to share with you are tools that work for me personally and that have helped me transform my life. Maybe you know nothing about me and you've never heard of my best-selling audiobook – *Paul Mort Will Save Your Life*. In that book, I share not only the story of how I turned my life around so I could have a positive impact on the lives of thousands of people, including the friends, colleagues and family closest to me, I also share the stories of people

I've worked with who've achieved the same, people that show my methods work.

This material is not based on theory alone, it's going to be heavily practical. You might have already read about goal-setting and habit-building. You have probably downloaded audiobooks or listened to a few podcasts, perhaps watched a few YouTube videos about the power of intention. However, it's one thing understanding it, but completely different actually executing it. Knowing and not doing is the same as not knowing.

None of the routes to upgrading your life that I'm going to share are any use to us unless we develop consistency. I find the best way to do that is to start with a positive morning routine, building on it with well-established habits, and that way we keep to our sense of purpose and focus. This is a method that you can commit to every day – meaning, you wake up each morning with a sense of opportunity not anxiety.

Upgrading is about preparing for the shit life throws at us and the way in which we respond to it; teaching you to find wins in your life, making it hard to feel bad and easy to feel great. During times of adversity and challenge you don't rise to the level of your expectations, you fall to the lowest level of your training – and we'll be fight-fit thanks to a regimen of journalling, meditation, visualisation and reflective training. You can't always be in control of events, but when you're in control of your thoughts and reactions, you will always be in control of your life. When you're used to being in panic mode it becomes habit to respond to even the smallest upset like it's a full-scale emergency. It's part of what makes life full of confrontation and stress for so many people. Upgrading means letting go of so much of that. I'll teach you how to make peace with the mind's natural tendency to overinflate problems beyond the scope they merit.

And we won't do it alone. We'll dip into some ancient Stoicism too to give us a framework with which to approach difficult, seemingly impossible situations. This Greek and Roman philosophy tells you how to brush the shit off when it hits your fan and how to move on with dignity, free of your critics. The philosophy is still around after 2,000 years, and there's a reason for that. That's another part of the Upgrade process – it's about building on good things, improving and refining – not criticising everything that's gone before. We are going to be future-focused, looking back only to learn, not to stagnate. I'm going to introduce you to some modern-day legends too – some of the experts that open up my mind so they can do the same for you.

You are going to learn how to become masters of your time, so that blaming someone or something else for your tardiness becomes a thing of the past. We'll look at how we create big energy in a positive way with everyone around us and with anyone we meet.

What emotion is holding you back from getting what you want, and what do you need to DO to smash through it? You'll learn how to kick self-doubt out, and how to smash 'overwhelm' in its tracks, moving beyond it with elegance and ease.

Developing the *Upgrade* mindset will enable you to stop feeling shit and start feeling more like your true self (who you might not have met for quite some time!). It's time for a fresh look at the way you approach things when they aren't working out. I'll give you the 'no bullshit glasses' that allow you to see through the old unhelpful stories you tell yourself and get back on track with laser-like precision to where you want to be.

Prepare to live a life less ordinary. I speak from experience, and I walk my talk; I live a life which *is* less ordinary; working a four-day week, taking four holidays a year with my family, turning my phone off in the evening and at the weekends and spending as much time as I can with the people I love – my wife and kids. And yes, I sweat my swinging bollocks off to be able to do that. Fortunately, I love what I do, and so will you once I help you make the jump to the place where you operate from joy rather than subservience to a life and situation that you hate.

Before we start, let's take a look at a definition of Upgrade.

> *Improved or made more efficient. Desirable and high value. Reorganised, updated, modernised and reformed, promoted, raised or boosted.*

This my friend is where you want to be. Thank you for buying this book, now let's kick some dick!

How to Use This Book

The *Upgrade* method isn't about building robots or copies of me – it's about using your strengths to their maximum effect. If you use this book in a way that works for you, you'll be getting your own custom-fit method to master your mindset.

Are you a feaster or a grazer? If you like one big kill then to go away and digest it, by all means race through the book and then go and think about what stands out to you, what you're going to think about and what you're going to do. I hope you'll come back to the chapters, advice and exercises that are going to help you make the changes you've identified.

But most of us change our habits by showing up daily. I've started each chapter with what I call a 'mind vitamin'. Think of this book like getting a daily shot. You might think you've not got time to read a book, but just give me one day, and read one chapter, do one set of the questions at the end of each chapter. Asking questions of yourself controls where your focus goes. We can all make time for that.

A chapter a day to change your life? Sounds like it's time to get started …

Unfuckwithable – What is it?

Mind vitamin

In 2014, I was in Dana Point, California, in a conference room with 800 other men. The course I was attending was called 'Wake up Warrior', and as part of the programme, I initially had to fight another participant on the beach in order to dispose of both of our egos so we could move forward in a humble way. Remember, at this stage I was at rock bottom and I had seen pretty much every shrink in the land, but the things our coach, Garrat J. White, was advocating – like the ninety-day, challenge-based lifestyle, meditation, and introducing me to Byron Katie (who we'll learn more about in a later chapter), really inspired me and that year I went on to make my first million quid.

The next course run by Garrat that I went on was in 2016, and was called 'Warrior Week'. Part of it involved all of the participants assessing where we were in life. For some reason, a new venture I'd started just wasn't growing, I'd plateaued for about eighteen months. I knew it could work, though. My Eureka moment arrived when I realised that there were specific things holding me back: I was worried what people might think of me setting this new business up, and so I wouldn't make calls because I feared rejection and that people would laugh at my idea, and criticise me. In that session, I realised that if I wanted to grow I had to be prepared to be laughed at and criticised;

to embrace the negative possibilities but get through it by developing a thick hide so the barbs that might fly at me would just bounce off. The cost of entry ticket for making a success of my new idea demanded that I become Unfuckwithable.

At the time, I'd been sitting on a video I'd made eighteen months previously. And with good reason, I thought. In it I disclose a searingly personal account of my lowest time: panic attacks, binge-eating, suicidal thoughts and porn addiction – as well as my reliance on cocaine and booze. For ages I'd been undecided about going public with the video, which I'd made to inspire others, to reassure them I knew where they were coming from as I'd been there myself. But I was shitting myself with what the fallout would be; what if my mum or somebody else in my family came across it? I also feared the negative comments that would come back at me. But that Warrior Week wake-up call made me certain I had to post the video. And you know what? At first, I thought I'd been right about all my fears. After I posted it, plenty of fuckwits commented that it would have been better if I had jumped off the cliff after all. Nice, eh? But I had to look beyond. The overwhelming majority of comments I got – and there were a multitude of them – were positive, grateful and encouraging.

My first step to becoming unfuckwithable was the realisation that even the hideous comments that I received from trolls weren't half as bad as the ones I'd imagined. If I hadn't taken the big leap into the unknown and posted that raw, truthful video (which, btw, has now had over five million hits), and if I hadn't prepared and braced myself for the shit that losers would throw my way, I wouldn't be writing this book right now. There's a saying: 'The higher you soar, the smaller you appear to those who cannot fly.' There will always be jealous fuckers, people who criticise you because they know they don't have the minerals to attempt to do what you are achieving. Upgrading is knowing that you're going to get criticism, but if you know what you're doing is the right thing, going ahead and doing it anyway.

Self-acceptance/self-knowledge

Upgrading is about not fighting who you are but learning to be at peace with yourself, acknowledging your insecurities and your imperfections and moving forward from that place of acceptance. And if you're reading this and thinking that you're incapable of considering yourself in a positive way, take heart; I was a functioning addict, beyond miserable, right off the fucking scale. It was because my self-esteem was so low that I found myself stood on a cliff like an Acapulco diver. You really have to have lost total belief in yourself to go *that* far, because thinking of stepping off a cliff only happens when you feel worthless and have given up on you and the world around you.

Unbeknownst to me, my wife, Lesley, had followed me to this macabre spot, and she was stood nearby, nervously watching, desperately wondering what the hell to say to get me away from the edge.

'Think about the kids,' she said.

'I am thinking about the kids, and they are better off without me.'

She's a quick thinker, my lass, 'Okay, then,' she said, 'imagine them being referred to as the kids whose dad killed himself. How do you think they will feel?'

That was what cut through for me. *My kids*, what the hell was I about to put them through? Some people aren't lucky enough to have someone there who can help them find that cut-through moment. Some people have problems – medical or practical – that they can't see past in that moment. But in that split second, I saw through mine. Since then, I want to make sure other people never get as close to that ledge as I did that day. What it gave me, though, has changed every day since.

Stood a hundred feet above the rocks below, something dawned on me that would change my view of life forever – I and I alone, had created my current state of misery by my behaviour, negative thoughts and feelings. But what if I flipped it? I wondered. If I could create this mess without thinking, what could I create with positive intention? Suddenly, I felt as if I found the key to the meaning of life. When I looked at my life in a cold, forensic light, I could see that one negative event had triggered another negative event and I had unconsciously been drawing misery towards me. Positive attracts positive, negative attracts … well, in my case, utter shite!

Oddly, that lowest moment for me was what made me wake up to the power I had. I'd put all of that energy and time into negative thoughts and behaviours, but I could reverse it. To do that, I knew I needed to think big. I needed more of a destination than just 'the opposite of where I was'. I needed a plan about where I wanted to go, and to get there, I'd have to picture it.

I had to teach myself to visualise. And do so with positivity and generosity. It's a habit I've not stopped since. I visualise not how much I *need* to earn, or where I *need* to get to, but how much I *want* to earn, and where I would *like* to get to. I visualise not what I *need* but what I *desire* – because now I can trust that my desires support my goals not undermine them. I live in a state of gratitude, wonder and abundance, all because of that insight, which came to me before I was about to meet the Grim Reaper by jumping off the cliff. If you can imagine what you want in life, you're halfway there to making it happen. We'll go into this in much greater detail later in the book and we'll consider the science behind it.

A map of the world

I've touched on how I had to work out where I wanted to get to if I was going to save my life. The problem is, even if you and I picked the same destination, we've got different maps. That's why we each have to decide our paths ourselves. We all have a unique map of the world that represents the way that we live our life and see our place in society; what we think of other people and the set of values – or lack of them – we have been taught and operate by. We add to the map with our experiences as we move through life, sometimes changing our opinions and cutting and pasting, and generally making a right old fucking mess with the glue to create a mosaic of what we *think* is reality. Very often, what we think is true turns out to be utter bollocks, an old story we are still telling ourself, one that no longer serves us. We're reading an old map, one we drew ourselves and looks nothing like the real road ahead. The voice that tells us we are shit, which the brain lazily backs up with old 'evidence' (that can go back to when we were wearing shorts in school!) gives us an excuse to never push ourselves beyond the place we are in – that voice is looking back at the old map. Upgrading is about seeing these old self-limiting maps for what they really are and replacing them with ones based on who you are today and where you're going.

We are all doing our best, but it often seems like some of us are having an easier time than others, and while anyone can tell you not to waste time comparing yourself to others, some people actually are having an easier time of things. And you want to know why? Because they have got to know themselves and what makes them tick. And more importantly than that, they've cut themselves a bit of slack. I don't mean they're letting themselves slack off – the opposite, in fact. It means they're not wasting energy hating who they used to be. They've put some faith in themselves to be able to find the right direction to head in. I learnt to respect myself because no one else could do it for me. If you don't respect yourself, believe me, no other fucker will. And it didn't happen overnight; I stumbled and fell quite a few times, but yes, I finally learnt to cut myself some slack, too. If the me on the ledge had learnt that, it might not have taken my wife's words to get me to take that step back. But it's a prime example of how a step back is sometimes a step in the right direction.

This isn't to say it's 'job done' for me, now. Remember, we are all works in progress and constantly need to develop our inner selves, and this requires self-respect and discipline. Being alive means growing. We need to revisit what we believe in and what we expect from others on a regular basis. Upgrading means not just tolerating, but welcoming change.

If you want to make your present better, make your future bigger

So, I'd had the wake-up call, I'd learnt I had to draw myself a new map, but how did current me make the jump to future me? I had to see them as connected. Future me wasn't different – I was Upgraded. Even a tough moment in the present is made better by knowing it's a step on the way to a bigger future. Planning isn't always about the tough stuff either – it can be fun things to do with your friends and family too. Design your goals around a purpose that means something to you. And if you create challenges and timelines of when you will complete them, you'll find you generate a kind of electric excitement that will power you – and others around you. We'll explore this more in later chapters, but think of it like you've got this huge energy source within you – you just need to find the switch.

Where I place my attention, I direct my intention

It was a revelation to me that this power was free. I didn't need time or money to tap into it, and we can all use it to energise us. Excitement can be created on demand by our thoughts alone. I used to think of thoughts as airy-fairy stuff – useless compared to action. But since I learnt more about the neuroscience of how we think and feel, it's unlocked the value of powerful, intentional thinking. When we think, our brains are alight, signalling to our hormone centres which produce corresponding feelings. We are what we think. Be aware of your thinking at all times. Remember, 'where attention goes, energy flows'. Too often we tend to think our thoughts are inevitable – a flow we can't control or influence. But stepping up means engaging in active rather than passive thought. And it's not just about adding in positive action – you can choose to limit the negative ones too. Say, for example, you've just broken up with your partner, allowing yourself to endlessly think about them will just make your brain reproduce old feelings and pretty soon, you will be overwhelmed. I'm not saying you ignore those thoughts – but ask yourself, are you thinking things through, reaching new understanding or decisions – or are your thoughts just in a holding pattern or spiralling? The latter are the ones you are allowed to cut off. Process, don't wallow.

My pal, Rich, my co-author on this book, separated from his girlfriend and got so fed up with how quickly his thinking was polluted by regret and sadness with no corresponding progress or action, that he started wearing an elastic band on his wrist so that each time he found himself pining for her, he gave it a good stretch and let it twang back on his wrist. It's a good way of keeping on top of the kind of negative thinking that leads you only further down a dead end.

Triggers

Sometimes you can stop negative feelings before they even happen, especially if they are outdated – habits rather than real thoughts. Most of us know the different way our minds work when we're thinking through a new problem compared to the mental chewing gum of just going over old ground.

The trick is to be super aware of what just happened in your thinking and what triggered the shit feeling last time you had it. Maybe your trigger is a place, or familiar scent that you associate with your ex. Sometimes, just being aware of the trigger can take away the feeling. It's like you've found it and rumbled the thought. Peace and progress come from tackling the issue at the centre, not just letting the same thought run through your mind like the kind of hold music you get when you're trying to talk to the tax man.

As you'll see over the course of this book, we've got fuck all control when it comes to pretty much everything in life beyond our thoughts and actions. Given that isn't a great deal of control, it makes it all the more important that we learn to understand the one thing that we can control: us! So enjoy mastering what you can: the way that we choose to be; how we handle situations; our opinions; the values we stand by and our response in the face of adversity. Understand yourself and you can be in the driving seat when it comes to all of those. I'll admit it's a tall order because to understand ourselves, we'll have to learn to override many of our instincts (that have been rooted within us for hundreds of thousands of years) and question our thinking. But once you have learnt these techniques and can apply them, and you begin to know yourself better, it's so much easier to live the life you want.

We have a choice about how we feel, we really can reclaim our power from negativity and despair. 'What you give your attention to, you add momentum to.' Please forgive me if I sometimes sound like one of those motivational posters, but I love some of these phrases! Find one that nails it for you and come back to it. I like: 'If I don't seek out challenge that inspires me, I will attract challenge that drains me' to get me moving forward.

You need to take radical responsibility for where you are right now, and set yourself challenging goals and an exciting vision of the future. Stop waiting for something or someone to do it for you. You have the power: an average human brain has around 70,000 thoughts per day. Imagine if you harnessed even a small percentage of those to serve your goals.

Exercise

1. Write down the way you want to feel, your preferred state – whether it be happy, positive, empowered, confident, self-believing, joyful, appreciative, grateful … all of these can be summoned by our thoughts, and the feelings we generate ourselves can be just as real as the ones we experience brought on by outward circumstance.
2. Practise triggering positive feelings and excitement. Write down five things that give you an inner smile, so you can use them to flip negative thinking.

The Electric Life – Living a Supercharged Existence

Mind vitamin

One of the reasons I was stood on the edge of that cliff having suicidal thoughts back in 2014, was because I had no sense of purpose. I had stopped moving towards things I wanted. The only thing that excited me was getting drunk and snorting cocaine. Rinse and repeat. I thought I'd made it, so I had given up on creating any new missions. I asked myself:'Is this it?'

Living an electric life is essentially about having a compelling vision that you are constantly moving towards. It means having the kind of goals that give you a buzz just thinking about them. And it's the kind of energy other people want to be near. Being around people who are excited about moving towards their goals is unbelievably inspirational. It will make you want to help them and achieve your own.

Allan Stone was a barber and a very good friend of mine. This wonderful guy had it all; he was always excited, always in a rush and was always late! When I had my hair cut by him or when I trained with him, he was always the best part of my day. He seemed to just radiate positivity. Allan passed away suddenly at a very young age, and I struggled with his death – it had me thinking about my own mortality. We were both the same age, his kids were the same age as mine. But he had been so positive in life that I knew I wanted to follow his example and live life with that same energy.

Death is a hard thing, but we can take lessons from it. We know it can happen to any of us at any time. The problem is, we never think it will. At every funeral you go to, people will always say, 'Life, it's all over in a heartbeat, it is so short and precious.' But that's just lip service, most of us never actually do anything about it as a result of this brief brush with death. Instead, we slink back under the warm duvet of comforting denial and sleepwalk through life. Then one day, claimed by illness or old age, we suddenly wake and realise the gift of each new day and all of its limitless opportunities; but by then it's too late and that's the day we see the figure with the fucking cloak and scythe tapping softly at the window.

When you get to the end of your life, imagine lying on your deathbed thinking, 'I wish I'd asked that awkward question; I wish I'd been brave enough and asked that person out; I wish I'd visited that country that I thought was too far away; I wish I'd started that business, and quit that job that I disliked so much. I wish …' Do you know that the yearning for having taken more risks in life, is the single most common regret people have before they die?

And that's definitely not for me - a life full of regret for things undone. It doesn't stop you fearing things – criticism, failure, knockback – but we can stop that fear holding us back. Better to have tried than lived in quiet desperation, which ultimately ends in deep regret.

So let's create an electric life, not a boring one, so at the end of it, instead of thinking, 'I'm kind of glad that's over', we see a life lived in all its richness and diversity, one that was full to the brim with joy and love expressed. I want to close my eyes looking back on my life as if I'm watching a movie – I don't mind a few twists and turns, setbacks and battles, as long as I get to the end credits and think, 'Jee-sus, what a ride I've had!'

Power up

An electric person is somebody who is charged up with energy and excitement, with a face that lights up with enthusiasm, and the imprint they leave on others is to make them feel energised and more positive for being in their presence. Easier said than done, though, right?

It's normal to be tired, upset and not to feel amazing all of the time. But what if you could get up every day and summon those feelings of excitement? And what if that excitement was on tap simply by picturing your vision of your future? You are where you are right now as a result of the thoughts and habits you have adopted in your life. To feel excited, pumped, ambitious, *you* need to change your habits; you can't just wait for it to happen.

Habits are powerful things. They're behaviours which take us into autopilot, which is great if it's a positive habit, but if we've built in something that's not in our own best interests, the power of habit means we sometimes don't even realise we're doing it. The key here is waking up to these bad habits. I know that if I let enough of them catch up with me, I could end up on that cliff again, so I try to be conscious of all my habits – good and bad. You have an option, you can either water the flowers or water the weeds; focusing on what is good rather than bad. The consequences of habits are there for all to see. All the results you currently have in your life right now are indicators of your past behaviours and current habits. What you are doing right now is an indicator of your future results, so it's only today that matters.

Once a bad habit becomes established it can still be removed, but it takes persistence. As it does with new habits – in fact, they're only truly habits when we stop thinking about them actively. New results require new habits, and new habits require us to take on new behaviours; we have to change our perception and thought processes and our actions. Don't leave it to hope or wishing. Hope is empowering, but it's definitely not a strategy.

Mind and body connection

Our physiology is how our bodies function – it's where we're at physically; be it our posture, our circulation or how much oxygen we're taking in. It's how we *feel* physically. It's hard to look after either your mind or your body if you can't understand how they interrelate.

Our mindset needs physical support, just as our bodies thrive when we're in a strong headspace.

I'm not here to make simplistic judgments on what physical or mental health is. Most of us can recognise when we're suffering on one or both fronts. Upgrading isn't about reaching some unattainable standard – it's about incremental improvements. But I do think there's a lot of problematic language around the health of our minds and bodies. 'Mental health' can span everything from a bad day to a lifelong clinical condition, so let's not use it as a lazy catch-all. For instance, and you might not agree with this, but I think that when somebody is very low in themselves often it is not depression but rather that their energy is absolutely rock bottom. Sometimes depression is not depression at all, it's just burnout from doing too much or putting your focus on negatives. Likewise, if you are in a state of clinical depression, while you're getting support, you can begin to work out if it's your circumstances or your mental landscape that could benefit the most from change. I really believe that depression is not something that you possess, we shouldn't say *my* depression, like it's a dog that's leashed to us and we are forever stuck with it – no, depression is a state we can pass through.

When you look at some of the bloody awful things some people have to face – tragedy, illness, loss, poverty – on the surface it can seem wild for me to say 'suffering is optional' but I do believe that. We can't stop shit happening – but we can fight against the urge to feel shit about it. In fact, some of the most inspiring people I've been lucky enough to meet are people who have either been through, or are even still going through, some of the worst things life can throw at you. But they are somehow still finding a way to inspire others and finding an inner energy. I see that impact on their physical self as well as their mind.

Great physiology is not about having a six-pack, but rather it's about feeling connected physically, knowing that when you take a deep breath in you feel the power it can bring you. Upgrading your physical state is about where you are and where you want to be – I'm talking personalised goals. It's about building on what you can do – can you get moving, can you get outdoors, if you do that already what's the next goal that excites you? If you're suffering from chronic health conditions that restrict your options, then I'm not going to pretend you can make everything better – but you can focus on what you can do rather than what you can't. Your energy can be impacted by the way you are holding yourself and what you're thinking.

Whether I'm exhausted or not, there are some things in my life that give me energy. These are different from the fairly universal things I think we'd all say give us joy or fun, they're specifically work, goals or plans that power me up – I call them my batteries. For me, some of the main ones are teaching, training and coaching. Yes, they're outputs for me, but they also energise me, as does jujitsu. I get excited from just focusing on them. There are activities that will energise you, too, if you think about which of the ways you spend your time fill you up rather than drain you. The mind and body are inextricably linked, and where our mental attention goes, our physical energy flows. Energy is everything and, yes, we should try to give it a healthy habitat – looking after our sleep, our nutrition and so on – but we don't have to just wait to receive it. If you want to Upgrade your life, you need to remember we've got the capability to generate positive energy like a power plant. Energy is simply the capacity to do things – but when you lock on to the fact that it doesn't need to just be neutral, that you can make that energy a positive thing, it's a superpower.

If you're feeling fucked, you have to look at what you did yesterday to make you feel like that. A lot of my friends complain about their lack of energy, but you only have to look at what they did at the weekend? Spending two days pretty much pissed. That's going to destroy your energy. How can we expect to feel great when we treat our bodies like shit?

And I get that life can be busy so you might not have the time, money or space to go off and work on yourself, but you can find the positive energy in what you are doing. A weekend with the kids? Yes, there might be chaos or rushing around or bickering but also notice the moments of happiness and joy, the love? We experience them in our body. Let yourself feel it.

Or you might be on your own, or fighting the kind of mental battles I touched on earlier. People with overwhelm or anxiety have their own particular physiology. It might be tight shoulders and sweaty hands, or tense muscles and shallow breathing. Depression has its own physiology, it can make us slump-shouldered and slower in movement. You might not be able to remedy your depression instantly, but you might be able to roll your shoulders back, release your jaw and stretch your muscles. You're letting your energy build again just by changing your posture.

Brain hack to positivity

To break the chain of anxiety or well of depression you might be spiralling into, force yourself to smile and keep smiling for two minutes. Physiologically, what is happening is that the specific facial muscles it takes to smile signal to our brain's emotional centre that we're in a good mood, and our brain – not knowing the difference between us bullshitting or us feeling genuinely happy – gets the steer that we're okay and then gives us more serotonin and dopamine to back up that mood. The more that we practise smiling, the happier we become. It's very difficult to smile and think of something negative at the same time. Give it a go! I'll bet you my used jujitsu jockstrap you can't do it. If you keep smiling, the chemicals in your body direct you back to something that makes you happy. This trick of the mind is massively powerful if you're feeling anxious, down or are suffering from low energy.

Chemical reactions

If you can start to build simple exercises like these hacks into proper, sustained habits then you're setting up a positive feedback loop. The energy you project, even the optimism and confidence in your voice and body language, will cause a chemical reaction in you. Good habits will start to change the biochemistry of your mind and body. I'm no neuroscientist, but I think all of us can feel the difference between those good, natural hits of dopamine we get when we connect with someone, when we move our bodies or hydrate properly, compared with the artificial hits we get from junk food or the endless social-media alerts on our phones. Chase the real stuff and it will grow.

The results in your life can and will feel different every day because of your ever-growing levels of energy. It's like looking at the world through different lenses. When your energy is higher your confidence is also higher and you're ready to take on challenges. But I'd be a fool if I told you it is just one mindset flip and you're done. The real trick is sustaining that mindset and energy through obstacles and setbacks. We are social animals, so once we can create great energy, how can we protect it from threats from other people and our environment?

Our mind is like a newborn puppy. If left untended it will run wild, falling back on the only thing it knows, its instinct. Without your guidance the pup lives on panic and suspicion – always ready to fight or flee to protect itself. Because it doesn't get fed the right 'mind food' – no positive thinking, no self-affirmations, no self-control – it will feed itself with whatever's available: typically old crap from the first available dustbin. The mind goes feral and the puppy ends up being more like the wolf it evolved from.

But when the mind is taught discipline through guidance, it can grow into a fine companion that works with us. If we feed it the right happy thoughts, it won't panic as it now knows where to go and what to do. It will always have some of the wolf in it, that's nature, but all we have to do is understand the way it works and keep it from falling back into its fight or flight state.

Start looking at your environment. For a lot of us that means the people we spend our time with. Pay attention to who's in your WhatsApp groups, who you hang out with. Environment will always beat willpower. Upgrading isn't meant to be a battle. Make it easy to make good choices.

I think a lot of us have stopped striving for what we really want. You're going to hear this a lot throughout this book (repetition is sometimes the only way I can get through my thick rhino hide and probably yours too!), but we have complete agency to determine the richness of our existence – that's not necessarily agency over circumstances, but it is agency over how we experience and interpret them. It's down to what we envision, then strive for, while really believing we deserve it.

I often come across people on my coaching courses who are unable to picture anything positive in the future because they're so blocked and unhappy in themselves.

People who stand where I was on that ledge are often people who no longer see anything of any value in the future and therefore have nothing to live for. If I come across a person like this (and they are largely men), I ask them, 'How do you want to feel?' and that begins to open them up a bit. The answer I usually get is, 'I don't want to feel like this.' If you can't immediately get to what you want, start with what you don't want, but crucially, keep going. Next, I'll ask, 'What emotion do you want to feel?' And then, 'Why is that important to you?'

Don't let your brain tell old tales

One of our brain's jobs is to put things into context – effectively making sense of the world by building a story around events, our feelings and experiences – it links things together, helps us recognise patterns and saves reassessing every situation by telling us a story about what happened last time. This way, it helps justify our current emotional state, providing a reason and context for it. In other words when we feel a certain way the mind tries to explain *why* we are feeling like that. That's why we say things like, 'I feel stressed because of my job.' 'I am depressed because I feel like my business is failing.' The trouble is, sometimes it links the wrong things together, or tells us an old story that's out of date. Sometimes, it even puts big emotional stories around our feelings, which might be temporary or purely physical. What if circumstances aren't as bad as you're telling yourself – but actually you're just tired, run-down or not looking after yourself? A problem that seems insoluble today because you're knackered, stressed or poorly nourished, will probably look much more solvable tomorrow after a good night's sleep. We'll go into this in greater depth later, but it's a great reminder not to always believe the stories we tell about ourselves. Don't confuse feelings with facts. Try the checklist below to see if your mood is affecting how you see the world.

Recognising signs of low mood and low energy

When you are tired and your energy is low:

- Your perception of your success and where you are in life compared to other people is skewed.
- You are more likely to self-sooth in a way that's actually self-sabotage.
- Your confidence is lower.
- Your intolerance for other people is higher.
- It triggers even more stress.
- You are less likely to take on challenges.
- You start to believe increasingly worse things about yourself – you probably tell yourself that you are lacking motivation when actually, you're just lacking energy.

I recently put on three kilos in a month whilst I was trying to lose weight. My energy was low and that meant I was less likely to eat well and work out. That's a pure paradox, as you'd think I would want to take care of myself to get better. I knew I could either believe the bad stories I could tell myself around this situation, or I could remind myself that I had the power to raise my energy on demand and change how I felt in an instant by using the affirmation, 'I'm always gaining control of how I feel and I can change it in a heartbeat.' For me, that means raising my focus to my goals, doing the things that charge my batteries and paying attention to my physical state. It worked. I got my energy back and got myself back on track.

Consider how lucky you are to be the best part of someone's day, to be able to make a real difference. Ask yourself:

- If I was able to generate more energy, I'd be more likely to - - -
- If I was able to raise my energy who else would it impact?
- Who needs me to show up and have a powerful impact on them today?

Hug it out

If you still find you can't find a way to bring yourself into a state of positive energy for your own goals, then flip your thinking. Do it for someone else. Most of us love to feel significant to somebody else. We can be the best part of someone's day. And as selfish as it might sound – if you want to feel good about yourself, do good for someone else. One of the fastest ways you can start to feel significant and valuable is by making someone else feel special. And don't worry if you're not a hugger. It doesn't have to be a physical hug to make somebody feel appreciated, you can tell them verbally, write on their social media, send them a WhatsApp, a text, or gift. If it's a colleague, you could say thank you with a little Post-it note, you've written and stuck to their computer screen. Think about how great it makes you feel when you're paying it forward, thinking less of yourself and more of other people.

I'm telling you right now, do this every day for 100 days and your life will transform. Over 101 days, I wrote on my wife's Facebook wall 101 things that I love and appreciate about her, even tiny little things. It didn't just make her feel good, it made me feel great, too, and our relationship grew.

Appreciation is more proactive than gratitude. Gratitude is the lubricant of positive flow, training your attention, but appreciation is making sure someone knows you're grateful. Think about when somebody has made you feel great by something they have said or messaged, a little video they've sent perhaps. Don't you want to pass that feeling on? If you want to feel significant raise somebody else's significance – send them a note, voucher, or message. We can get too stuck in our own little worlds and think we're interrupting people but actually if you take the time to tell people when you're impressed, grateful or inspired, you're powering up both them and yourself at the same time.

Meditation

If you need to build up to putting yourself out there, there are other ways you can build your energy, and meditation is one of the most powerful and accessible. Some people think meditation is about emptying their mind of thought. I disagree. It's more than that. Meditation gives you a stillness and peace in which your creative self has a chance to deliver you insights. Practise it regularly and you will see not only the mental benefits – but physical ones too. Done often, meditation leads to the body producing lower levels of cortisol (the chemical associated with physical and emotional stress). It also helps us sleep, lowers blood pressure, heightens mood and improves general brain function. It's also good for your immune system. It is said that twenty minutes of meditation is equivalent to four hours of sleep, and I'm not suggesting that you try and pack forty minutes of meditation in instead of going to bed at night but it gives you an idea just how powerful it is. Meditation is a great response to panic attacks and stressed states as it roots you in the present, where happiness lives, here in the right now.

There's no right or wrong way to meditate, no secret knowledge or equipment required. Find what kind of meditation works for you:

- Guided meditation, like you might find on apps like 'Calm' or 'Headspace'.
- Ascension meditation which I did with the Ashire monks.
- Transcendental meditation.

Personally, I don't enjoy guided meditations. I like to focus on my breath, or say a mantra, focusing on my third eye between my eyebrows. I find I need to do it for fifteen minutes per day to get the benefits. I do mine first thing in the morning on my acupressure mat, which has plastic nails on it that I lie on. I know other people that put their headphones in meditate their way through their commute. We often rush through our mornings but taking the time to spend even ten minutes like this can power you through the rest of your day.

Energise

Once you've got your head in the right place, your body should follow. This could involve going to the sauna, getting out on your bike, doing some burpees, or just taking a walk. Moving your body is great at any time of the day – but if you can make it part of your morning, you're going to maximise the benefits. Most people have a cup of coffee and a shit and just go straight to work. Then they wonder why they can't handle the pressure – it's because they don't put themselves in the right state. And after you've got moving, get hydrating. Without water, your thinking will be fuzzy, your body more sluggish. It's one of the simplest things we can do to keep our energy levels where we want them.

High-voltage friends

So, what is a high-voltage wake-up call? It's an emergency, one that shocks and shakes you to the core, scares the hell out of you and makes you re-evaluate everything. And while it might scare the absolute shite out of you when it happens, a few weeks or, most likely, months down the line, you may realise it's the best thing that could've ever have happened to you.

These can come in many forms: panic attacks so real that you think you're going to die, chronic depression which gets you thinking you want to take your last breath, a near miss that makes you realise your reliance on substances could finish you off.

I wouldn't wish them on anyone – but if you are in that place, and I've been there – then take courage from the fact that their purpose is to terrify you into waking up out of your sleepwalk and then reset your vital systems. It's a bit like scrubbing off all the crap that's accumulated on your computer's hard drive and restoring factory settings.

When you make peace with these dramatic high-voltage friends, you'll begin to realise that you can make even life's scary moments work to your advantage. They're warning signs that you and the time you have here is precious, and you should value it just as you are also valued. Let the high-voltage wake-up call burn off your misery and let hope back in. You see, although humans are programmed to catastrophise constantly, our inner wellbeing and sense of joy is like a beachball pushing to get to the surface of a swimming pool; it is our thinking that stops it getting there.

Alarm clocks

If you've not reached the point of a high-voltage wake-up, there might be other alarm bells ringing. Anxiety and depression are often alarm clocks that alert you with direct feedback from your body.

The stress you hold in your body should be listened to. If it's hanging around, ask yourself:

- What are you doing that makes you feel this way and what makes you think that that's the way to do it?
- Is it habit or circumstance that's brought you to this point?
- How have you allowed yourself to reach the point where this has become normal?

You have to get to the meat of the problem, and not let the stress become a background noise that you adjust to and start to ignore. What are you currently focusing on? Are you overthinking the job interview that didn't go well, or the partner you split up with months ago? Or maybe things are OK right now and yet you are worrying about what may happen, creating shitty visions of all the things that can go wrong?

People are obsessed with the past and future when in truth, the one place where they should be sucking the juice out of life is in the present, despite the fact that most of us spend very little time there.

Imagination is a race horse and it can gallop away from you if you don't keep control of it. The brain is a problem solver so you need to keep it busy, challenging and directing it. In order to live an electric life, I need to know exactly what I want in order to find my excitement today. You need something to chase. If you don't seek out positive challenges, something to work towards, you'll end up with challenges that drain you; or even create them just to keep your worry muscles flexed. Life always finds a way to remind you that it's about growth and not complacency and will do what it needs to take you to the right place. Being stuck in a comfort rut is where so many people are and sometimes stress is a sign that you need to climb out of that ditch – before a high-voltage wake-up calls forces you out.

Information without action is consumption. Society has grown fat with self-help books but unless we do something practical to bring that wisdom to life, they are worthless.

Pretending

Do you not know what you do, or do you do what you know?

What are you pretending you don't know so you don't have to do the work? An example of knowing what to do but not doing it, is losing weight. People know how to lose weight, but they believe that the pain of staying at the same weight is less than the pain to change. Once the pain of doing the same becomes greater than the perceived pain of doing the work, that's when change happens.

This might be triggered, for example, when you see a photo of yourself and you think, shit I really am overweight. It's a dose of reality, a wake-up call. I went on holiday to Tenerife not long ago, and I felt really uncomfortable with my bodyweight. It was the first time in about four years that I didn't feel comfortable enough to wear a pair of budgie smugglers. I couldn't tell myself I didn't know how to tackle the problem – I was pretending I didn't know what had gone wrong, pretending I didn't know what the answer was. Once I'd dropped the pretence, I could get on with sorting the solution.

Batteries or black holes

Is what we are doing giving us energy or draining us? Hopefully after this chapter you'll have a good sense of what charges your batteries, or have been inspired to try some of the new ideas here.

Before you move on, check you're clear on the following:

- How do you raise your energy?
- How do you want to feel?
- How do you not want to feel?
- How do you want to act?
- How do you not want to act?
- Which area of your life could you increase the reps in?

Exercise

Answer the six questions below to boost and focus your energy.

1. One word that would describe the feeling I want to create today is . . .
2. The reason I chose that is because . . .
3. One thing I'm willing to do to create that feeling is . . .
4. What one thing am I most excited about today?
5. Who needs me to be unstoppable and have a positive impact on them? Is it your daughter, your son, your wife, husband, colleague?
6. If I could raise my energy who else could it impact?

You're Just a White Belt – Silencing Self-Sabotage

'A white belt may not be a black belt, but it's a higher rank than sitting in a chair.'

Mind vitamin

There have been many moments in my life when I have felt inadequate, where I have thought I'm not good enough. Whether that was when I was starting my business, being a husband to my wife, a father to my kids, a coach to my clients. When I ask on my Instagram 'What single thing is the biggest limiting belief that is holding you back?' The most common answer is 'I'm not good enough'.

That belief can become a crutch, a chorus and then ultimately a road-block – a reason not to go forward. My next question to a person claiming this is, 'How do you know that you are not good enough? Where's your proof?' And there's never a good answer – either a feeling or a piece of old history – never a true obstacle.

The next question is what actually is 'good enough'? Can you see that you can never reach a standard if you don't know what it is, so instead you keep on telling yourself you're not good enough. Forever.

There's an opportunity here to see the impact of question framing. You have two clear options:

- *When you ask, 'How do you know that you're good enough?' you're setting clear, measurable goals, and when you can answer 'Yes' to the question, you know you have met the required standard and the facts tell you that unquestionably, you couldn't be where you are without being good enough.*
- *If you ask yourself, 'How do you know that you're* not *good enough?' you need a follow-up question: 'What do I need to do to reach the desired standard?' This brings you back to positive focus and gives you a clear goal, a strategy, and direction to head to a very specific destination.*

In 2014, I was still drinking at the weekend. I was also taking lithium to control my bipolar condition, which would then sap my energy, so I'd have a gram of cocaine during the day as a pick-me-up, and at the weekend too. Something had to change. Around this time after a friend of mine got his boxercise license, he asked me if I wanted to practise on the pads working on punch combinations; it would be good exercise for me and good practice for him as a coach.

After a couple of weeks, he asked me if I fancied a crack at putting all those punch combinations I'd learnt into action, with a real life person opposite me doing full-contact sparring. 'Great,' I said, 'let's do it.' So, my opponent punched me in the face, and I punched him back. I thought to myself, *Yep, this is for me!* The danger element of boxing and adrenaline that my body was releasing gave me a similar rush to that of cocaine, so I have boxing to thank for getting me off the Colombian marching powder. I am forever grateful for that. I'd replaced a negative with a positive. The only problem was, I was getting the shit beaten out of me by lads in their late teens and twenties, who trained every night and didn't have jobs or parenting to worry about. Because of work strictures and family life I was unable to train to the level I needed, getting regular sparring in so I was ring-fit and developing my skills. Instead, I kept getting my nose broken. Better than the coke, but still not exactly sustainable.

At the time my son was into jujitsu, so I thought I would try that instead of boxing. I threw myself into it as much as my busy working life would allow, but again I could only train a few times a week, as a result of which I felt I wasn't developing quickly enough. Pretty soon, that sabotaging voice that tells us we're crap, started saying, 'You're shit at this, you're still just a white belt after six months, so just give it up.'

I started listening to my inner critic: 'Maybe I'm not getting any better?' I asked myself. 'Am I good enough? I'm being tied into knots by lanky seventeen-year-olds, maybe this is not for me, and I'm just shit?'

I sent my coach a message – *Mate, I don't think I'm going to come back, I feel like I'm not getting any better at this, if anything I'm getting worse*!

His reply was simple, factual and it stopped me in my tracks. *You're not shit, you're just a white belt.*

I rethought about it in those terms – a white belt is just someone who has not done enough training yet to become a blue belt. If I wanted to grade at a higher level and move up then I had to put the time in. It wasn't that I was shit and not cut out for jujitsu. When I took the emotion out of it and looked at where I was in practical terms, a white belt was just somebody who is on their way to a blue belt, it's up to them how quickly they get there, depending on how often they train. In other words, cut yourself some slack, you've just started.

My friend, the writer, James Smith, started learning jujitsu around about the same time as me and within six months he managed to get his blue belt, whereas it would take me three years to achieve the same. A year later, I went on a course with Conor McGregor's coach and he said, 'A black belt is just a white belt who didn't quit.'

Self-soothing

When people talk to me about self-sabotage it is usually within the realm of self-medicating – often drinking, substance abuse or porn addiction. It's easy to label them self-sabotaging behaviours, but I think that even we know they're damaging, we don't do them to deliberately harm ourselves. I think we 'self-soothe' to make ourselves feel better in the short-term, doing something which isn't in line with us chasing our goal, or being who we say we're trying to become. It's only afterwards that you label it as self-sabotage. At the time you're doing what you can to feel better, even if it's a line of coke, or smoking or you're falling off the clean-eating wagon. Obviously, in a wider context, there is such a thing as self-sabotage, where somebody's esteem is so low that they don't believe it's worth attempting whatever their goal might be, or they think they don't deserve it, but most of our self-sabotaging is actually an attempt to answer a need in us. If we can pause long enough to ask what that need is and lift our focus to our long-term goals, then that pause is often enough to make better choices without feeling like we've denied ourselves anything. You're just investing in the future, upgraded, you.

Look for the wins

Instead of giving myself a roasting for not having a blue belt, I should have realised that just showing up for a jujitsu class, given my responsibilities, age and busy life, is in itself a win. Instead of berating myself for being submitted (when you tap your opponent to release you from a hold and therefore lose) or because I'm tired, I should reframe how I measure success. Instead of only measuring forwards, thinking how far we've got to go, we should remember we can also measure backwards and look at how far we've come. In this instance, instead of being down on myself for not having a blue belt, I had to remind myself I had lasted a round with a brown belt, five whole minutes without being submitted!

We need to recognise the positives because our inner voice will automatically feed us the negatives. If you're climbing a mountain, you don't just keep looking at the summit and the agonising distance that you've still got to climb, because that will break you mentally. Sure, you know where you're going, and you keep taking glances, but instead, to really feel progress, you put one foot in front of the other and every so often look back at your footprints to see just how far you've come and how well you're doing. It's about being your best possible coach. Positive self-talk is fucking important, it's the foundation of future success. There's a big difference between delusional self-bullshit and recognising your achievements and giving yourself encouragement to spur you on.

Don't be a perfectionist

All too often we create rules that set us up to lose. We confuse progress with perfection. People only think they've done a great presentation if it lasted exactly the time that they said it would, or they didn't forget a word, or all the apparatus worked perfectly. I no longer judge myself negatively if I forget a few things, fuck up the slides or go over time a little. It's not about lowering your expectations and standards, but about recognising progress as opposed to perfect progress. For instance, my goal this quarter while I was writing this was to get my weight down to 80 kg. I didn't get there, but I did reduce it down to 83 kg. And I did this with a torn pec, during a time when I had two holidays and had to deal with a staff crisis. It wasn't perfect. But it was progress.

Jujitsu is a difficult measure of progress. When you're lifting weights, you can measure how many reps and sets you've done and what weight you're lifting; just as in business you can see your balance sheet and your sales. When you can measure your performance, it gives you a clear idea of whether you're progressing or treading water, because when you know you're progressing it gives you a natural lift to keep showing up, and push on because you know it's worth it.

But as with juijitsu, it's not always obvious. I've learnt to have a different criteria for success. I don't measure myself against others anymore, but instead ask myself how can I get to be as good as them? What are they doing that I'm not? Some people say that comparison is the thief of joy, because when you look at others and see their outward success it can make you feel like a loser and as though you should have done better. Remember, comparing what you know about yourself with what you think you know about someone else is never going to match up. We do it all the time on social media these days, but it turns out we've been doing it for millennia.

Plutarch was a Roman dude who lived 2,000 years ago – don't ask me for specific dates! – and who wrote a book called *Lives of the noble Greeks and Romans*, which weighed up their strengths and weaknesses, comparing a Greek leader like Alexander the Great, with a Roman like Julius Caesar. The idea was not just to capture history, but also to do it in a way that meant ordinary people could model some of their behaviours and beliefs to self-improve. There's a fine line between comparison and inspiration. Comparison is where you assume you're comparing like with like, and finding one side wanting, but inspiration? Well for me I'm not expecting the people who inspire me to be perfect, I'm not expecting me to be exactly like them – I'm locking on to particular skills or characteristics they've shown, not trying to turn myself into a clone of them.

The way we frame things that happen to us and attach meaning to these events controls our experience. In 2020, I had two clients who were both originally from Dublin and both of them ran gyms. Then, because of COVID-19, gyms were shut down. By the end of the pandemic, one was making more money than he had before the outbreak, while the other one went out of business. The first gym owner pivoted and took advantage of the situation, thinking to himself, *the community needs me more than ever.* He let people know he was going to stay accessible, that they were going to train by Zoom and he was going to be consistently there for them. The latter slumped on the couch and thought, *I've got no choice but to close my business down*, giving refunds to his customers before he even asked if they wanted a different kind of lockdown service.

Both gym owners were facing the same situation, the difference between success and failure was the meaning they attached to it. For one, it was an opportunity and they grew their business faster than ever; for the other, all he saw was a dead end.

Just a little postscript to this story. Back in the early days of Zoom there were a few teething issues with security and privacy and anyone could jump onto Zoom. *Anybody!* One of the tutors was doing an online workout and noticed that they'd been joined by a naked man who was busily knocking one out! So it's not that the first gym owner had it easy – he had plenty of challenges to face and situations to adapt to – but he faced them with the belief that his plan could work.

It's this habit of looking at your end goal that can help us not fall apart at the bumps in the road. Sometimes it's worth looking at the bigger picture and reminding yourself that the thing you're currently stressing about, when compared to something life-threatening or really tragic, is not worth the energy. Just remember that what you are worrying about now will probably not be taken to the grave with you!

It's who you know ...

Hopefully, you will be alert to your own urge to self-sabotage now. But as I said before, you're not in this alone. There is no such thing as a self-made person – there are always figures in the background who helped and advised them how to get where they are today. The cheat code to success is not making all the mistakes in the book, but instead seeking out those who have already made the mistakes and who can advise you how to avoid them.

How do you become more magnetic?

There are a number of things that charismatic – magnetic – people have in common:

- They are open and curious toward other people.
- They are interested in helping others without looking for something in return.

- They water their relationships by regularly checking in with friends and colleagues and by being emotionally available for them.
- They make you feel like you are the only one in the room when they're engaged in conversation with you.

How many of these characteristics can you see in yourself?

Exercise

Make a list of ten success stories in your life you were directly responsible for, then write each one in detail; what you did to make it happen and how you felt when it worked.

How to Survive Without Social Media

Mind vitamin

Instagram, Facebook, TikTok, WhatsApp, Telegram, YouTube … social media is a funny thing. It almost feels like it's taken over the world. It's certainly taken over people's lives. It's an opportunity for us to show off, consume and create. Sadly, when you overdo it, it tends to be depression that it creates, as well as anxiety and fear.

Of course, social media has plenty of positives – the communities it builds, the connections it can forge, the careers it can build. And unless you're a drug dealer, and I've known quite a few of those in my time, you'll need social media to grow your business. There has never been a faster way to get in front of your perfect customer. But here's a couple of tips for you: first up, ask yourself this simple question, 'Would you say your primary use of social media is to create or consume?'

Like a raiding party I like to get into my social media sites quickly, then create, drop and leave. I drop my posts, photos, videos and my content, and then I get the hell out of there. How many times have you picked up your phone to do something useful – and then gone down the rabbit hole and got lost?

I have a great life hack to make my phone less appealing to me – I stick it on black and white mode and this alone has halved my screen time.

So, I now get the benefit without the drawback. If the black-and-white screen trick doesn't make the difference to you, try a lock-out app. 'Freedom' and 'Cold Turkey' are two apps that can help you block out social-media websites on your phone. I've also heard of people who've basically started treating their smartphones like our old landlines – having them in one place to use them as a tool but then when they need to switch off, leaving them at home and just using a 'dumbphone' – a brick that just does calls and texts – when they want to be offline.

I'm not asking you to beat yourself up if you're hooked on your phone. We all feel the pull of them. After all, millions of dollars of research has gone into making them, and the apps they carry, as addictive as possible. And it's not that they're inherently bad, more that they encourage us to break our boundaries. The problem is that people gorge themselves on social media, they're bloated with doomscrolling. And who really needs a whole shopping mall in their pocket 24/7? It's basically just over-consuming. You become mentally stuffed, but because you've been grazing – snippets of content rather than anything in-depth – it starts to mess with our focus too. Not only do you start comparing yourself to the people in and on your phone, but it encourages a strange kind of envy. You might find yourself asking, 'Why haven't I got that?' rather than asking yourself, 'How can I get that?' or being grateful for what you already have got.

And that's without touching on the anger so many of the websites we visit trade in. A lot of news websites have worked out that rage keeps people scrolling, so they offer you ever more extreme news and content. Is that what you want to fill your mind with?

Since 2018, I go on family holidays without my phone so that I can be completely present with my wife and kids, not wasting my time arguing on X with some random dickhead. I remember once seeing this guy and his son in a park. The kid was trying to get his dad's attention but his dad was ignoring him whilst busily texting with a pissed-off look on his face. Finally, he hissed, 'Go and play!' to the boy. Imagine your hero being more interested in what's on a screen than you. Poor kid. But it's so easy to be that guy.

When I started going on holiday without my phone, it actually made me more organised because there were things that needed to happen before I went away. It made me get better at delegation and let go of the need to have control. It made my team level up because they knew that they could not contact me.

And of course, phone addiction isn't just a bad habit. It's a gateway to an expensive one. The idea with all of this stuff is to get us hooked on these platforms and then later start charging us for them. And the big tech companies get paid twice by us – they get our money, for subscriptions or storage or commission, but then they get to harvest and sell our data too. And are they looking and listening to everything we say with a deeper darker purpose? Well yes, I'm afraid so, as that's exactly what happened with Cambridge Analytica; information about us was sold on to companies who bought the analytical data so they could more specifically sell us things we would buy.

We are so trusting as we enter these adult sweetshops with their sparkly window displays, that we're oblivious to their invisible jaws as we step through the door. It's not just the theft of your identity, it's what spending time on these sites does to you and your children.

Facebook, X and Instagram were all set up at the beginning of the twenty-first century within six years of one another, so while there's sufficient science-based data studies to prove beyond question that those people who use social media excessively are more prone to depression, anxiety and a lack of self-confidence, it's far too early to know what the long-term effects are. And even though many of us are aware of this, we still find ourselves enslaved to our phones. The addiction is like slowly sliding down a steep slippery hill, being fully aware of it happening, but unable to stop it. We look around us and see other people as dependent on their phones as diabetics are on insulin, and we realise that we're *all* sliding down that bloody hill.

Most of us baulk at the idea of coming off social media, even temporarily, despite the fact we resent scrolling through clickbait and blindly searching for something that we know we will never find. The lure of social media is its promise of instant gratification, so why then does it leave us feeling empty? The promise of the experience is always better than the reality. We know that social media, like some modern Mephistopheles, offers us unhealthy voyeuristic glimpses into others' lives, which in turn make us feel there is something lacking in our own, and yet still we use it. We seem to forget that people, often us and our friends included, project an idealised version of themselves on sites like Instagram and Facebook. Now, with the aid of apps that allow you to change the contours of your figure and sharpen your jawline and cheekbones, you can tell a story about yourself which just isn't real. And even if you don't do that, are you occasionally guilty of selecting a filter which makes you look the dog's sparkly bollocks, one where the colour saturation is jacked right up? We've probably all done it. I applaud celebrities like Hugh Jackman who, rather than adding to the mountain of unreality we're all trying to climb to the top of, posts un-doctored pictures of himself looking like shit (like the rest of us lesser mortals) just after he's woken up in the morning.

By placing ourselves on public view we render ourselves vulnerable and sensitive to the comments and opinions of not only our real friends who we see and make physical contact with, but also those virtual so-called friends and followers, many of whom we don't really know. Coming off social media isn't easy if it's been a constant in your life.

Most of us get up in the morning and shower and start our day only after we've had a quick scroll on a few sites to see what other people have said, or check our own posts in the hope they might have been reacted positively to. And sadly, these are the same sites that we also look at just before we turn off the light and head to sleep.

The way we *begin* and *end* our day and the thoughts we feed our brain just before we close our eyes are very important, because anxious or fearful, depressed or angry, these emotions inform the happiness level with which we start the next day, influencing the unconscious way we feel about ourselves in the world around us. If you're feeling down or anxious, these feelings will be magnified tenfold by visiting social-media sites.

Social-media addiction is defined as excessive use of social media leading to negative consequences in a person's life, including problems with relationships, work, school and mental health. The first step to surviving without social media is recognising the triggers that push you towards it. Think about the times when you use it most; what's the feeling that has pushed you there, is it loneliness? Boredom? Procrasination? Each time you feel the urge to pick up your phone for a non-essential activity, try to replace the action of scrolling with something else that is a little bit more positive, like going for a walk, doing some stretches or reading a few pages of a book. We often finally throw our phone down when we're annoyed with how long we've spent scrolling – yet no one ever tells me they wished they'd done fewer press ups, read fewer books or drank less water. Use the good habits to fill the gap your social-media habit leaves.

A friend of mine's girlfriend recently came off Facebook and felt so much better for it, but in order to activate her business account on Facebook she was required to have a personal account too. As soon as she recommenced giving any information about herself, she noticed that she was experiencing higher levels of anxiety. She also noticed that when her mood was dipping she would return to her Facebook page hoping that somebody had left a positive comment because it gave her an immediate uplift. It's hard to put anything on social media without feeling like you're on some kind of fishing trip, waiting for a bite.

What is actually happening with these sites is you are taking a risk each time you place something out there for all to see – be it an opinion or photo – you're laying yourself open to other's scrutiny and waiting for their praise, indifference or dismissal; a congratulatory badge of recognition, a public display of affection en masse, in order to help validate yourself. And when you get that recognition, like a dog receiving a treat, your brain releases a dopamine hit which makes you feel instantly better. This might be okay, but sadly, each time you receive a 'like' or a positive comment you are becoming increasingly addicted to this quick hit. And the longer you stay on social media the harder it is to get your fix and the more treats you need to feel the same way.

There's a scientific term for the stress and anxiety we initially feel in the absence of using social media, it's called 'neurobiological withdrawal', essentially, the fear of not being constantly connected. Classic FOMO. Not being able to access social media is known to lead to an increase in cortisol release by the brain. Cortisol is the stress chemical that so many of us in the modern world are producing on a low-level constant basis, and social media together with the stresses of modern life are directly to blame.

Essential to a productive day is having a good sleep the night before. Scientists have measured the levels of sleep of those who use social media and compared them with those who don't, and the amount of restful sleep a non-social media user experiences is hugely more than that of someone glued continually to their phone. A lack of sleep, on a continual basis, leads to a diminished immune system, which can have direct correlation with serious illness – from depression right through to cancer.

It's not just stress levels that social media increases, it also puts your wallet under duress. Think how many pop-ups specifically geared around your browsing history are waiting for you every time you turn on a social-media app. It's not just like we choose to go onto a shop's website now. Instead, advertorials and sponsored content sit alongside ads that track us and our likes and dislikes; every time you scroll through there's a tempting sale from your favourite brands waiting for you. And because most of us buy almost everything online these days, you're just one click, one retail-dopamine-push-of-a-button away from receiving that sparkly product which will be delivered to your door in no time at all. A staggering forty-nine per cent of Millennials interviewed (according to Schwab's 2019 modern wealthy survey), said that as a result of social media they felt themselves influenced to overspend on both experiences and products.

Another thing that really bothers me is cyber bullying, and it's not just kids who do it, but adults as well. Trolling is the act of intentionally instigating conflict online in order to antagonise, humiliate or isolate someone. Its effects can be devastating, attacking someone's self-esteem, sometimes leading to self-harm, thoughts of suicide and, in the worst cases, individuals actually taking their own lives as a direct result of being subject to it.

Our homes were once safe places away from bullies. When you closed your front door you were safe from the world and your antagonists or abusers, at least until the next day. These days, there's no respite. Trolls and cyber bullies are waiting for you as soon as you're online. Unless of course you turn your phone off. There is always that option. You wouldn't knowingly let people into your house who were unpleasant or ignored you on purpose, so why do you let them into your mind?

This is exactly what we do when we give our time to social-media sites that leave us feeling empty, dejected, persecuted and ostracised.

Ever since the pandemic, many of us are working more at home in our own personal space than we are at the office. During lockdown, social media was a great way to communicate with friends, it brought people together virtually in a way that wouldn't have been possible without it. And to be fair, for some people who live in the middle of nowhere, having access to Facebook groups is a way that they can be involved and get some support. The bottom line is if you work from home then the likes of Instagram, X, TikTok, WhatsApp and Facebook will all negatively impact on your time and the quality of your work.

How to withdraw from social media

When you take a break from social media, sure you'll maybe experience a little FOMO, but in a very short space of time you will realise that you're not missing out on anything special and you'll probably notice so much more going on around you as you are more fully invested in the present. But if a complete digital detox feels like too much, you might first try a holiday from your accounts over an agreed timescale. Say, one week. It doesn't feel drastic if you know you can go back to checking them in a few days. And by the end of those few days you might already have started to cut the cord. During that newly available time you'll find you now have, try and direct your interest into a hobby or project, something that you can be proud of and that feeds you in a positive way.

One really easy win if you're not ready to go the whole distance yet is to switch off your notifications. Yes, you'll probably still end up scrolling too much when you do check your accounts and timelines – but they won't be pushed into your attention constantly. You might think you can ignore them, but research has discovered that if you get an alert that you have a message, a like or a notification and you're not allowed to access it, your anxiety levels start rising. The problem with receiving push notifications is that these constant interruptions prevent you getting in the flow, and every time we stop it gets harder to go back to our work or book we are reading and refocus. It's not just the time we spend on these sites that we lose – it's the time it takes to get our mind back to where it was before the alter. We end up lacking time and doing a half-arsed job. The overriding takeaway from having spent an hour on Instagram is we don't really remember much of what we've been looking at, and the reels (even the holistic self-help ones) are so bite-sized that there is little substance to any of it. Perhaps you think you've found a genius tip, and you dutifully save it to watch again later, and to try it out. How many times do you actually end up cooking those recipes, doing that exercise, using those storage tips that you've saved?

Whereas, spend an hour doing something which requires sustained creativity and attention and by the end of it you get a sense of satisfaction of something produced, something that you can account for that time spent.

Another helpful thing you can do if you're not ready to delete your account completely, is start making a note of your screen time. In other words, being tech-mindful. Most smartphones will give you an indication of how much time you've been looking at these sites every week. Make a note of this and start to consciously scale back that time, replacing the screen time with something that gives you pleasure. Also reward yourself for doing this. In a short space of time you will have replaced the habit with a new reward system.

And just as we explored earlier how being around inspiring people will motivate you, the same is true here. An interesting suggestion from the Centre for Internet and Technology Addiction is that if kids are excessive in their use of tech, very often it's because the parents are too. And we know overuse is connected with depression. Because if you're on your phone too much, you're not physically interacting with the people around you and that's how we really build our energy. The next time you reach for your phone, think about upgrading your life rather than your devices.

How to tell if you're a social-media addict

The American Society of addiction medicine defines addiction by five factors:

- The inability to consistently abstain.
- Impairment in behavioural control.
- Craving.
- Diminished recognition of significant behaviour and interpersonal relationship problems.
- A dysfunctional emotional response.

When you start lying about your screen time and it starts interfering with your relationships, that's when you're addicted. The truth is, social-media apps were designed by behavioural scientists who made the experience so smooth and pleasurable that you would return to them again and again because you were addicted to the feedback loops, notifications, likes and the instant validation. So, we are now all clear that the reason they went to all this trouble was not to make you happy, but rather so you'd spend a long time enjoying their sites, giving them sufficient time to present you with ads which they could make money out of, data they could monetise. Not a great deal has changed in recent years, we are still subject to the use of cookies and tracking of our browsing habits, the time of day we tend to use social media and the things we look at. The difference is that nowadays we have to agree to that in the small print. Have you noticed now on Google that before it actually performs a search for you, you have to agree and accept their terms?

Do you sometimes experience that crippling feeling of shame when you're in the company of your favourite person in the world but you still find yourself looking down at your phone and scrolling to see if you've had a message or a like? My friend you're not alone, but know this: taking a social-media detox for even just a week is the mental equivalent to decluttering a flat full of rubbish. You will also be establishing a foundation of discipline to build on as you continue to eliminate other weaknesses that you want to address.

It also pays to warn people that you're detoxing so that they can support you. Many who sever their connection with social media report feeling a sense of relief, and figures show that most of them don't return to these sites having experienced a renewed sense of freedom away from them.

The best way to go cold turkey is to delete the app on your phone that enables you to access your account, and deactivate it permanently. Yes, it will feel weird, and doubtless you will get the urge to log back into your account just in case you missed that special something. But eventually, by replacing dead time spent screen scrolling with stuff that you should be getting on with, like taking care of your health, spending real time with your friends and putting important hours into your work, all these things will soon begin to impact positively on you.

Exercise

1. Would you rate yourself as more of a consumer than a creator?
2. Do you believe there are more downsides than upsides to using social media?
3. What are the top three actions you could take to make social media work better for you?
4. List the top three things you could do to give yourself an enriching break instead of picking up your phone.

'Great Story, Bro' – the Bullshit We Tell Ourselves

Mind vitamin

Other people tell stories about us, just as we tell ourselves stories. And unless we dust our story cupboard on a regular basis, we can end up limiting ourselves to believing stories that are now obsolete and no longer fit for purpose. Like when somebody you haven't seen in years, cracks a joke about how disorganised you are. Well, maybe you were years go when you were at school with them, but you're forty now and run your own successful business, so that story just doesn't fit anymore. Perhaps the teller is threatened by how much you have evolved, while they have stayed the same. We have to filter stories about ourselves before we accept them. We also need to check the bullshit levels we feed ourselves. My co-writer Rich noticed how quickly he repaired his self-mythology when he got a boxing lesson in the ring; he was temporarily humbled with the self-knowledge he was a gutsy but very average boxer, but within days he'd sufficiently recovered his over-generous opinion of his abilities.

Then there's the story about my fear of rollercoasters, which until very recently I told myself and 100 per cent believed, even though, and get this Mush – I had never ever been on a rollercoaster before! They just looked like something I wouldn't enjoy. In truth, I thought that I hated all adrenaline rides. And for years my mum kept watering my near phobic-level fear of heights and confined spaces, all based on one very old episode; as a child I'd gone on one of those fairground shuggy boat rides where you're packed in like sardines, and as the boat swings like a pendulum you think you're going to drop out. That was the old story I, too, had been believing, and it had slyly grown to a fear of all adrenaline rides. Even though the evidence of my personality was that of a person who loved taking risks, be it with investments, sky-diving, in jujitsu bouts and full-contact boxing; all these facts spoke to the contrary of what my mum and me had been feeding my brain all these years. By rights I should love rollercoasters!

So, guess what? The last time I took the family to Dubai on holiday and wanted to join in with my kids having fun, I decided to test the old story to see if it really was true. They were going to ride a terrifying rollercoaster with more twists and loops than an episode of Luther. *In the queue, my palms were sweating and my heart beating quicker than it should have been. This was my body expressing anxiety, or rather terror, at the perceived danger it was about to experience! It seemed like the old story was true, after all.*

But then, as we climbed aboard and I distracted myself by watching my kids' delighted smiles, evidence of them enjoying themselves, and the car raced off, I experienced a very different emotion to fear. It was pure excitement, and I loved the fucker! These limiting negative stories we tell ourselves are crutches that permit us not to grow and to avoid something uncomfortable. What we desire is usually always waiting on the other side of discomfort.

'I've always been crap at learning the guitar,' is a self-limiting story and leaves you no room to change. Instead, you might say, 'So far, I haven't found the right teacher', or 'I've not made the time to do enough practice yet', or 'Now I've been to that gig I know I still really want to learn this skill'. Let yourself tell a new tale. How many fears of yours are based on old stories which are holding you back?

Story is the basis of communication; we're always doing it, whether it's telling somebody about what happened in our day or weekend, watching news stories, or when we're gossiping. After all, I wouldn't be writing this book and believing it will change your life if I didn't respect the power of story. We love to talk about the latest film we've seen with a brilliant ending and an unexpected twist. Actors are among the most revered people in society because they bring us stories that allow us to escape ourselves for a few precious hours. But you don't need to be in Hollywood to spin a yarn. We're all natural storytellers and never more so than with the stories we tell ourselves that provide the glue to bring together the millions of different experiences, opinions and actions that make up who we are. But how honest and objective are we with our version of events and is there more than a dose of fiction sprinkled over the facts that don't please us?

It's really important that we are mindful of whether those stories are serving us well or putting us down and limiting us. As kids, we may have been told repeatedly that we were something that was not true. For example, a teacher labelled us as stupid, as was the case with me, because at the time ADHD, which I have, had not yet appeared on the medical landscape. For all of us, these formative years affect the rest of our life, and an offhand comment from a frustrated teacher – perhaps one who brought a bad mood into the classroom with him – ended up being aimed at you and it's stuck with you like a thorn buried under the skin for all these years. You're stupid. Hear it enough times and you start believing it.

Our map of the world, the way in which we view which directions are open to us, is based on these stories. But as we grow, we can cast off old skins as we mature, which can cause discomfort to those who thought they had a fixed narrative of who we were. At school, I was the classroom joker, pursuing laughs for attention and recognition, the kid who was going nowhere apart from to detention. Then I changed my story, started pursuing what I liked doing and many people found it hard to accept that the kid at the back of the class who was always fucking around, ended up being the most successful. I don't equate success solely with how many digits you have in your bank account, although it is one yardstick of achievement. Much more important is how well you know yourself and that's something that self-accountability and self-examination have allowed me to do.

The stories we tell ourselves about ourselves also mould our interactions with others and the levels of self-respect we go through life with. They form the bedrock of who we are, and when those stories are revealed to be incorrect, it can shake our identity to the core.

Like the person who discovers they are adopted and their personal history is a fiction that's either been told to them or they've built up in their mind. Or the special-forces operative who experiences PTSD whilst in the field, their body going into such extreme shock that they can no longer function in a job that they know backwards. They may sell themselves the totally incorrect story that they are a coward for submitting to fear and start to lose themselves in a mind fog of self-loathing and doubt, rather than tracing where this physiological state came from and piecing together the factual events which led to this self-combustion.

Sometimes, we can get entangled in a vicious cycle caused by revisiting a particular story; like when a friendship has ended, we've been ghosted and we go through it again and again in our heads, finessing what happened in order that it becomes the other person's fault and not of our own doing. This is why we need to sense-check our stories – the ones other people write and our own. Often our ego gets in the way and demands rewrites of what happened so that the story becomes more palatable, and we reframe ourselves as the victim because we don't want to be the villain of the piece. But if we can become more aware when we're getting stuck in unreasonable thinking which constantly rehashes who did what to us and how it wasn't our fault, accepting that it's normal to tell ourselves stories which get us off the hook, that is the beginning of changing unhelpful stories, realising that they're not always based on fact. Later on in this book, we'll look at the work of US speaker and author, Byron Katie, who had a massive effect on the way I now look at other people, and how I hold myself more accountable for the narratives unfolding around me.

What story do you tell yourself about your life and why it is the way it is? When you're in a rut do you lay the blame for your lack of happiness on your kids, your partner or work colleagues? Or maybe it's the fact you didn't get the right start in life and had a crap education? Perhaps it is all the fault of an illness. Like when I was diagnosed as being bipolar as well as having ADHD, that became a big part of my story and I'd blame the condition and what it did to the way other people treated me for making me depressed. Truth is, I was behaving like a prick to other people but if anyone challenged me, I'd just think that how unfair they were being was because of my condition. To every therapist and shrink I went to I couldn't wait to tell my hard luck story. If I'd written a book back then, I'd probably have called it *Bipolar – It's Not My Fault*. What a shite read that would have been about a big-mouthed self-obsessed tosser who thought the world owed him a living.

When I admitted to myself that with all the things that were going wrong in my life there was one common denominator – me – it kick-started a change. If you've got a diagnosis of something like bipolar or bad depression, people are a bit nervous about calling you out on any of your bullshit, especially if you're the boss of your company and the man of the house like I was; nobody's going to step up and say it. But after I contemplated suicide on the Cliffs, thankfully a few people came into my life and challenged my bullshit, and among them was an amazing support worker called Donna, from the community health crisis team. With her help I was able to realise that I was the architect of all the things that were wrong with my life. It wasn't a get-out-of-jail-free-card to behave badly – some of my behaviours were due to my conditions, but some were just me. And I had to realise that I could change both of those. Basically, I needed to stop trying to change the world and other people, as the only thing I could reliably change was me.

First up, I had to stop telling the story that I was a victim of bipolar, depression, anxiety and panic attacks, as that story was making me powerless. Most illnesses are not static, and your story doesn't need to be fixed either. I had found I was asking, 'How can I hope to be happy unless other people change to suit me?' That just wasn't going to happen, so I was stuck. Given that it's easier to change yourself than changing the world, you must change your story. And when you change the story, you change your state. Taking charge of your story is the first step in taking control of your life. And who knows it might mean you do go on to change the world after you have the confidence of having upgraded yourself. You have to say to yourself, 'I am in charge of all of this.' I love the phrase because it feels self-empowering. It doesn't matter how much or how little you have – we all have our charge of something, from our breath to our mindset. Your personal power is transformational, if you take ownership of your behaviour, you can change your life and everyone will benefit. Car manufacturer, Henry Ford, once said, 'If you think you can or think you can't, you're right.' In other words, if you believe in yourself and you're realistic about your abilities, rather than delusional, and put faith in your commitment to moving in the direction you've decided on, you can succeed.

Exercise

1. Can you list three self-sold stories about a perceived weakness you have which may be based on old evidence?
2. Can you list three weaknesses sold to you by others – like my fear of rollercoasters – which may be based on an old, out of date story?

We All Need an Animal to Slay – Having a Purpose

Mind vitamin

Every week I'm honoured to get thirty to fifty messages from individuals who are lost, struggling or stuck in a rut, and it's getting them down. I'm also contacted by people with anxiety who are suffering from overthinking. They all have one common denominator when I ask the question 'What are you working towards right now?' And that is that they can't answer as they have no clear goal or destination to head to. Where are you going to go? If you have nothing to aim for – no mission, no target – you'll just go round in circles.

When I cast my mind back to 2014, when I was at rock bottom, this was me. I'd lost my sense of vision and with it, all sense of forward momentum. Purposelessness comes from a lack of goals, and no matter who you are or however famous, we are all susceptible to getting lost in the vacuum. When I spoke to Ant Middleton, James Haskell and the legendary Tyson Fury, they'd all had the same experience; they've all achieved enviably high levels of success, but once they had summited their respective mountain they thought, 'Now what?'

John Fury, Tyson's dad says, 'Tyson needs regular goals to head towards just to keep him occupied.' I think that's true of all of us.

When we don't have something to focus on that we want, we will automatically focus on something that we don't want. Remember, the mind – if it's left to its own devices – is a negative pain in the ass and needs a constant vigil to stop it going back to simple survival mode. We have to direct it like a naughty child towards something that will challenge and occupy it. My life changed when I reignited my passion and sense of purpose, setting simple goals, targets and outcomes.

There's a simple question to ask yourself regularly, 'What am I working towards right now?'

I'll finish this sermon with a few words of fire and brimstone from the Bible – 'Those without a vision perish.'

Be brave enough to live your vision

Our real purpose in life and the purpose that is given to us by our parents and society are often two very different things. For instance, you come from a long line of fishermen (not much chance of that around my local Geordie waters!), and you're expected to follow your father just as he followed his father, out to sea. Deep down, though, you know you won't feel the satisfaction you would if you were to pursue the secret dream you've always had to go to film school and learn how to be a film director.

For those intrepid individuals who *do* decide to break the mould and realise and pursue their inner purpose, it's the difference between feeling electric, authentic and switched on to your real passion, where the potential is endless, and feeling numb about what you do for work and the feeling you have sold yourself short. I recently bumped into an old friend I hadn't seen for going on thirty years. As teenagers, we both went for the same job, working for the local council laying pavements. He got the job, and at the time I was gutted, but laying pavements wasn't my ultimate desire and goal, it just seemed like a nice little earner. My pal is still laying those pavements, and good luck to him, but my passion and pathway is taking me in another direction.

Let's imagine you are that fisherman with an inner dream of being the next Scorsese. What first steps would you need to take to start building a pathway to doing what really excites you? Off the top of my head, to get the ball rolling you'd find out where the film schools were, how much they cost and which were the best. Next, you'd research timelines – when term would be starting, how long their courses were and so on. Just by starting this process, you would be visualising it happening, presenting yourself with a new set of coordinates to follow your true purpose. And in picturing it, you would begin to feel the excitement of a whole other possible existence, even though you don't yet know how you'll get there or afford it. The *feeling* is there in your gut, and this is what you must follow, (remember that science has now proved beyond doubt that there are more neurotransmitter cells in your gut than a cat has in the entirety of its brain!), so listen to those gut intuitions if you're lucky enough to feel them!

Once you've decided on your course of action, the universe has a way of filling in the gaps for you. A well-known philosopher who came from a long line of clergymen – and this might be a bit of an extreme example – not only decided not to follow in their footsteps, he went on to become one of the most notorious radical freethinkers of the twentieth century. Saying 'God is dead' was just the start of it. His name was Friedrich Nietzsche and on the subject of finding your purpose, he said: 'He who has a why to live can bear almost any how.' (i.e. the shit that happens to us). Always follow your why, no matter the amount of pain which comes with it, you will be able to endure it because you're living an authentic life.

In other words, to achieve what you want you might have to go through hell to get there, but you won't mind because your purpose will ensure that you can endure whatever challenges and obstacles are thrown at you, because you know it will be worth it. Think about the pain and mental torture that Marines and British soldiers go through in order to become special-forces operatives. Do you think they would put themselves through this absolute hell just for the fun of it? They do it because they feel the drive to get there and because it's a club so exclusive there are only a few hundred special individuals made of the right minerals to become members.

My pal Ollie Ollerton was one of the original staff on the hit TV series, *SAS: Who Dares Wins*, which mimics some of 'Selection' – the gruelling interview process that separates the men from the supermen, where just a handful get through to join the Special Boat Service or the Special Air Service.

Ollerton was caught on his first attempt at Selection because a half-cut farmer, whose wife had fed them, gave them away to the hunter staff. But on his second attempt at Selection, Ollie was doing very nicely and had nearly finished the 'Fan Dance' run when he keeled over on his ankle and broke it. Mindful that this was his final attempt at the Special Forces, and trusting that he had the necessary minerals to make it, he taped up his boot and ankle so tightly with gaffer tape he could just about hobble to the end of the distance required. His sense of purpose that he was going to join the elite was strong enough to override the immense pain. And he was right. Ollie felt satisfied on many levels in the Special Boat Service, he had that strong-knit camaraderie, the feeling that he was an integral piece of a larger elite entity, as well as the excitement of dangerous missions.

But he didn't stop there. Purpose isn't a one-time game. You might think that being in the best military team in the world would have been enough for this guy, but there was still a gap between where Ollie was and true fulfilment. He would find it eventually, but first he had to go through some real nightmares. Having left the Special Boat Service after six successful years, he hit rock bottom; without the direction and routine of the SBS his life unravelled. Like me when I was in Spain, still earning loads of money but unhappy as hell, Ollie went through a period as a security adviser during the Second Gulf war, where he was living in Baghdad in one of Saddam Hussein's old palaces, and was being paid by his employers in bricks of US dollars. But something inside of him was empty and lacking, so he self-soothed with booze and our old friend, the Colombian marching powder.

The spiral continued, until one day he was approached by an organisation that specialised in saving children from a life in the sex trade in southeast Asia. Ollie was perfect for the role. He operated extraction missions all on his tod, with no back-up and unbelievably, no firearm. He had a purpose and more danger than you could throw an Action Man at, just like when he was in the special forces, but there was one crucial difference: he knew he was really helping these kids and making a difference to their lives. Helping people has been his number one goal ever since.

Take the emphasis off yourself and place it on others

According to research, individuals who find their purpose live longer than those who lack one. In an experiment, one group of old people in a retirement home were each given plants to take care of while the other group were given nothing to tend. Interestingly, the old folk with the simple purpose of taking care of a plant experienced better mental health and improved physical vigour. Just the responsibility of helping *something* else took their mind off focusing on themselves and gave them a sense of satisfaction. Don't worry, I'm not saying your destiny is to grow a cactus or water some geraniums. But don't knock it until you've tried it – you never know where it might lead.

Viktor Frankl was an eminent psychotherapist who created a psychological approach to adding richness and meaning to his patients' lives called 'Logotherapy'. In his amazing book, *Man's Search for Meaning*, he tells the harrowing tale of how he survived the holocaust in the infamous Auschwitz concentration camp by finding meaning in his suffering. He did this through helping his fellow prisoners. Frankl didn't focus on the innumerable tragedies he faced: genocide was surrounding him, most of his family had perished in the gas chambers, he was freezing and malnourished. Yet he chose to focus on the manuscript he was going to write on his release, which would detail all the horrendous experiences he'd witnessed in the camp, and in which he'd share the valuable insights he'd experienced that would help people in their own lives. He observed that those who were most likely to survive were those who had a plan that they were visualising, something special that they wanted to do when they eventually left the camp. Just having that hope helped keep them together and gave them something to focus on. A 'why' strong enough to resist the 'how'.

Frankl noticed, too, that there were also those like him (offering his medical skills) who, rather than focusing on their own sorrow, performed deeds to keep themselves busy, deeds which benefitted others.

Frankl proposed there are three ways that we can find meaning in our life:

- Through purposeful work that gives us satisfaction and helps others.
- Through giving and receiving love.
- Showing courage in the face of suffering or difficulty.

While the Nazis could take away their lives, their liberty, their clothing, slaughter their families and shave off their hair so they all looked the same, against some remarkable individuals who would not be broken, the Nazis were powerless. Yes, they could beat their prisoners physically and take everything material away from them, but they could not remove the way in which individuals chose to respond to suffering. That freedom remained untouchable.

He famously wrote: 'Everything can be taken from a man but one thing; the last of the human freedoms, to choose one's attitude in any given set of circumstances … You and you alone decide what your life will be in the next moment. Man is capable of changing the world and changing himself for the better.'

Frankl is talking about visualising and deciding what you want to think, even in situations beyond most of our comprehension. He showed this by finding positives and hope in what will forever be one of humanity's darkest moments. What a phenomenal power – all self-generated, built by his mind when he had nothing else. We all need a reason to be, something to hunt down, what some people call an animal to slay. It's these passionate purposes that give us a sense of what marks us out as individuals. When we don't have something that we feel truly passionate about, with a challenge related to it on which we can focus our energies, we're like the hunter who has lost the trail of his next prey. He gradually loses his skills set for catching his supper and buggers off to the neolithic chippy for his tea. Either that or he dies.

Instead of feeling alive and self-possessed, when we lose or can't find our purpose, our energies are no longer controlled by us – instead, given free rein to do what the hell they like, they take over and drive us to rock bottom.

The ladder's on the wrong wall

At thirty-two years of age, I was living in Marbella, and on the surface of things I had it all. A villa, sunshine, no money worries. But I was five stone overweight, drinking too much and taking too much coke. In short, the ladder was on the wrong wall. I'd sacrificed my hobbies, my friends, my health and almost lost my marriage in pursuit of my old goal, earning lots of money and having the trappings of wealth. I wanted to impress others with how well I had done for myself, this lad from South Shields. When I got to the top rung and looked around, it wasn't the place that I now wanted to be. I had an 'is this it?' moment.

The real problem was, I had no real purpose left. I'd designed my company in such a way that it was working very nicely but it involved no real input from me, leaving me the space to get depressed and unmotivated. Space is dangerous, I was trying to fill my time and vacant mind with something negative. In 2014, my family and I left Spain to live in the UK. Shortly afterwards, I took that drive to the cliffs in South Shields in order to take my own life.

I've already told you how my wife saved my life that day. But afterwards Lesley blamed herself for my unhappiness and dissatisfaction with my life. It wasn't her fault, at all, I had become uninvolved with my life and had no sense of who I was, no direction. To try and make me better we spent thousands on private shrinks. Why was I sad – after all,

I had lots of money, I was still making lots of money thanks to my business model and subscriptions, so what was the problem? The answer was I wasn't working hard for the money, therefore, it meant nothing to me. I needed to *do* something that really mattered to me, something that was challenging and fulfilling that I could pour all of my energies into.

The first step was to acknowledge that a change in my life was vital. The psychiatrist, Carl Jung, believed that the best way to determine what we need to change is to take note of how often we are afflicted by feelings of regret, guilt, anxiety or depression. If these are regular visitors to your mind, then you need to identify and replace them with positive self-talk and actions. If you can find the source of the feeling, i.e. the thought that gave birth to the unease, depression, etc, you can then challenge the thought; ask yourself, 'Is it worth lugging it around with me?' If it's anxiety you are experiencing, are you magnifying it beyond its actual dimensions? We'll talk about anxiety a lot in its own chapter later in the book, but the first step is the ability to question it. We often say now 'I have anxiety' as a phrase that means we can avoid really looking at the causes.

Once you connect with how to upgrade your life, you'll constantly seek to develop yourself and improve. It won't seem like a chore but an opportunity. The people I've helped through my programmes leave with a very sure purpose and a clear mission that they want to achieve, and don't pander to their egos. They have goals that they regularly set themselves, but the reward is not just in the satisfaction of finishing them, but also the transformation they undergo during the journey.

Think of what you want as your destination. You'll need GPS coordinates to get there. You need to train your mind to keep focused as things don't work straight away, you have to have faith in the process. They say the devil is in the dosage, so break down your journey into 'doable' micro snacks. Don't make too many plans. We can plan for so long we never set off, if we're not careful. But with the plans that you do write down, put them into movable, changeable chunks.

Finding purpose

Ex Paratrooper, Chris Lewis, had a long history of depression, which was threatening to overwhelm him. As a single parent he'd been clinging on to raise his daughter. When she left Swansea to go to university, he was at rock bottom so he did what he always did to try and feel better: he grabbed his surfboard and – since his car had been nicked – he walked to the nearby Gower peninsula, where that day there happened to be a huge fucker of a storm and humungous great waves rolling in on the beach. Despite the danger, he climbed down the cliff face, the storm raging around him, and jumped into the water between the sets of waves. No one else was daft enough to go out in the water, it was suicide.

The first monster wave hit him like a freight train, holding him under and crushing his lungs so that he was almost out of air, but the following break between the first and second wave gave him just enough time to breathe, ready himself and start paddling towards the beach as it thundered towards him. Amazingly, he caught it and rode it all the way to the shoreline where it spat him out. It was the ride of his life. That moment, lying like a dead starfish in the shallows, he remembered his daughter's parting shot to him, 'Dad, I just want you to be happy. You have to go and find your happiness.'

No, he didn't decide to become a world-class surfer, or find God, but as he looked down the coastline an idea occurred to him: *I'm going to walk the entire coast of Great Britain, covering every island until I find happiness, and I don't care how long it takes.*

Suddenly, he had a purpose; to keep walking until he found happiness. And to this he attached a goal to help give him some accountability, and keep him on track; whilst doing the walk he would aim to raise £100,000 for SSAFA (Soldiers', Sailors' & Airmen's Families Association), the charity which had been so good to him after he left the British Army.

Two days later, he set out on his mammoth escapade with thirty quid in his pocket, a crappy old tent that leaked and some decrepit walking shoes that were a size too small for him. But he didn't care, he now had a reason to be, a challenge. 'I had a goal, I had a purpose, I felt good mentally and physically. If I'm honest, at this point, only an asteroid wiping us all out could have stopped me from finishing this walk. I was so focused.' He went on to say, 'I now understood why and how people become so successful when it comes to achieving their goals. You have to be very driven and want it so much that absolutely nothing stands in the way until you get there; essentially, never giving up no matter what.'

After six years of walking through wind and rain Chris finally finished his epic odyssey in the summer of 2023. What is equally amazing is that during the walk he met his best friend Jet, a lurcher who never left his side and was with him every inch of the way till the end; and Kate, his future girlfriend and the mother of his son, Magnus – who was also born on the walk. It's as if the Universe was rewarding him for taking a chance and following a dream.

His best-selling book is called *Finding Hildasay,* the name of the uninhabited island that he found himself alone on for a month during the Covid lockdown. It was here that he realised he had finally found peace and happiness from within by following his true path. You might think that there's no further to go after you've been a para or special forces, but purpose isn't a one-time thing. When you look at Ollie's and Chris's journeys you realise that who dares truly does win.

Always have a new purpose ready

Another great example of someone whose life hit the skids until he was able to find a new purpose, is Tyson Fury. His amazing comeback to win the world title from Deontay Wilder is the stuff of legend, but for the benefit of those that don't know the background, here's a quick recap of a story that is far from a fairy tale.

Up until 2017, Wladimir Klitschko had been the dominant heavyweight champion of the world for eleven years. Turning pro and beating Klitschko became Tyson's obsession. And while his friends were busy doing the things that teenagers do, Tyson used every minute available to fine-tune his boxing skills in the ring. For as long as he could remember, he had suffered from depression, and had always felt different to other people, but when he had a pair of gloves on it was as if he could express himself through boxing. The ring was a sanctuary to him, a place where life made sense. And so, with an epic battle to face and the luck of the Irish, Tyson eventually got a shot at the world title, and ultimately outclassed a weary, bewildered Klitschko to become the new heavyweight champion of the world. Sounds like a Hollywood happy ending? Not fucking likely, Mush.

Before the fight that day, his father had asked him, 'How do you think you'll feel when you win?' Tyson's dark response was, 'Very depressed.' And that's exactly what happened, almost immediately after the fight. Having dedicated his teenage life to becoming the heavyweight champion of the world, now that he'd achieved it, it seemed like an anti-climax. *What now?* he thought, *what should I do next?*

Tyson's next chapter was played out in the media glare. On a diet of cocaine, beer and fast food, the champ's weight ballooned from eighteen to almost twenty-eight stone. It was one of the most spectacular falls from grace in boxing history, up there with Mike Tyson's horrifying fate of being sent to prison for rape. Fury's hard-won belts were taken off him when he tested positive for drugs and he became increasingly paranoid and lost. It wasn't until he found a new purpose, namely, to whup the ass of Deontay Wilder, after he heard Wilder writing him off on social media, that the tiger within him began to stir again. This slur, challenging his ability, gave him the necessary rocket fuel to lose ten stone, get his head straight and step into the ring to face off with the most dangerous right fist on the planet; at the time, a then unbeaten Wilder had destroyed almost all of his opponents by way of knockout. They were to fight each other three times: the first a draw, the second and third bouts both victories for Tyson.

I was lucky enough to interview Tyson Fury on my podcast and we got on like a house on fire – given that we are both bipolar we had a lot in common – and he shared this gem of wisdom with me: 'A busy person with lots to do has no time for depression or anxiety. Whatever your potential, if you don't have a clear goal in life, a well-planned target to pursue, you'll sink. We all need a sense of purpose and goals to challenge ourselves. We're at our best when we're striving for something bigger than us.'

Wise words from a giant. However big you are, even a heavyweight needs something bigger than themselves to fight for. But more than just an aim, we all need a well-planned target. A dream written down with a date becomes a goal. When there is a gap between you and knowing what your purpose is it's very easy to lose your way. Purpose gives us a place to head for, a challenge, a game to play, a scent on the trail to follow. Purpose gives meaning to our lives and meaning is so important. People without meaning, without a direction of travel, feel pointless, disconnected and rudderless and that's a dangerous place to be, Mush, because you start seeking to bandage your inner emptiness with self-soothing approaches that lead to addiction; anything to get rid of that hollow, haunting feeling of not knowing why you are here. Lack of purpose can infect many areas of your life, increasing anxiety levels and damaging your mental health, and it can strike people who've already scaled heights, but it's something all of us can tackle.

Do you feel hopeless, as if the joy button has been removed, and where there were bright colours, black-and-white shades seem to have taken their place? As I've shown, the feeling can strike any of us when we've either not found our purpose or need a new one. But on my programmes, many of the sufferers up this particular shit creek without a paddle, are guys in their forties and fifties. Whether you're in this age category or not, there's lots to learn from them. Is this you? Maybe you've hit your target in your career and are thinking *now what?* Perhaps your kids have their own tribe now, and aren't as dependent on you as they were? The tight pack of friends you used to spend your time with seems to have disintegrated as people have moved away or moved on? Often, it's not a crisis that triggers the realisation you're at breaking point – it's a steady slide to this sense of pointlessness you now feel.

Because a lack of purpose makes you feel low and unfulfilled, it doubles down by removing you from the healing company of your friends and family. You feel you can't reach out, or have no one that could or should listen or help, and so the symptoms worsen. But even though it's the time we can least face the world, isolation is the worst thing for depression, as it means you're suffering on your own, and unchecked, you go deeper and deeper into negative thoughts which aren't true.

Start asking questions

When we start asking ourselves questions, we begin to get in touch with our real inner selves.

That famous quote, 'Know thyself' comes directly from Socrates, the father of all philosophy, and the Socratic way is all about asking enough questions of yourself in order that you get to know the real you, and so you get to the truth of the matter. Epictetus the Stoic philosopher wisely said: 'Men are disturbed not by things, but by their notions about them.' In other words, we're fucking geniuses at over-dramatising situations and turning molehills into mountains. Two thousand years later, we're still doing the same thing. Epictetus believed that most people sleepwalk through life, never truly holding themselves to account or pausing to see where they are and if they're going in the correct direction for where they want to get to. Now and again, we get woken up from this sleepwalk. When somebody close to us dies and we suddenly realise we're not here for ever, or maybe we get an illness which again makes us sit up and face reality. But for the most part, even after we're awakened, we're quick to fall back asleep into the (un)comfy zones where everything is predictable. You'll find out more about this later.

Exercise

1. To help you find your inner purpose, ask yourself the question – how do you want to feel or act? What will make you feel that way?
2. If we were to speak in six months what could you have done to make yourself happy? Remember, happiness is not all about achievement but also the focus and travelling towards fulfilment.

Top of the Morning – Establishing Good Habits

Mind vitamin

Scientist and author, Dr Joe Dispenza, says, 'The hardest part of making a change is not doing what you did yesterday.' Just like improving your diet – first add in more good stuff before you focus on cutting out the bad stuff – so, too, is it true that installing good habits in yourself is easier than avoiding existing bad habits you may have. This is because bad habits are easy, convenient, give you an instant result and in the short term often make you feel better (like sleeping through your alarm).

The challenge with habits is that the win or the positive-feedback loop usually takes longer to show up than it takes to form that habit. You need to bridge that window with trust and focus on your long-term goals. You have to keep believing in the value of the behaviour even before results can be seen.

Back in 2012, I wanted to make my business bigger. I had a supplements company and a marketing company and I'd heard about the benefits of sending daily emails but I just couldn't get into the habit. The problem is, we think habits have to be something we do daily, and then when we miss a day we feel shit and abandon them. I learnt a rule way back, and that is that if you miss a day, don't overthink it, just get back on it the next day, but don't miss two in a row. And instead of trying to do it every day give yourself a little wiggle room; make the habit something you will do almost every day.

In order to help me commit to this goal to grow my business through a regular mail out, I leveraged my fear of looking stupid with some accountability to my staff by publicly pledging: 'In the next 100 days I'm going to send ninety emails and they will all be good.'

You have to get clear on what the habit looks like. Set some objectives. What are the numbers around it. In my case I wanted ten new clients. Why? So I could grow my business so that I could buy my son more things and take him to cool places. And ninety was a great number for me – it meant if (when!) I missed a day I couldn't use it as an excuse to stop.

This is another jujitsu story. Don't yawn! I've been doing it since 2015, and for the first three years I'd do about ten classes per year. Part of the problem was I couldn't get into a routine, so again I publicly declared that I would do thirty-five classes in the next ninety days. This worked out to about three a week. As it happened I ended up doing fifty classes, which earnt me two stripes on my white belt.

We need a standard for the new habit, a watermark to reach or surpass, and it's important that the number is not perfection. A lot of people have bought ice baths but have stopped using them because they can't keep up the daily momentum. A habit does not need to be daily to be valuable.

I read this the other day: 'Early mornings are hard for everyone but when you're wide-awake, the world is yours.' Rig the rules of each morning so that you start the day with a win. It's funny how many billionaires seem to get up before the fucking cock crows! How does 5 a.m. grab you, Mush?! I'm not suggesting you need to do the same, but in order to get a head start on the day so you have time to journal, meditate and take an ice bath or cold shower, you're going to need to get your ass up and out of bed a little earlier. In fact, I'd recommend an hour earlier. I get up at 6 a.m. and it's not a big chore. I do it because I want to, and because I love making the most of my life. And to do this, I need to plan where I'm going each day, so my body knows to follow. Having a structure always beats winging it.

This hour is 'your time', when you check in with yourself and programme your thinking: what you want to happen today and how you want to feel. It's just like punching an address into a satnav – Destination Optimism. And once you start embedding this sacred hour into your morning, you won't want to stop because you become so much clearer in managing your time effectively. Obviously, things during the day might derail you, and you might have to get yourself back on track, but you are much less likely to get lost if you've already planned your day in the morning.

Somebody once said, 'Early is a priceless timepiece owned by the successful' and I think this is true. Otherwise, you find yourself waking up without time for a shower, getting dressed and going to work and you're caught in a dreamy treadmill of repetition. There's nothing dynamic about it, you've done it so many times and that's why your computer brain is on automatic mode and places you in a sleepwalk. But when we specifically make the sacrifice of staying in bed for an hour less, something happens to us; we focus our minds on what we want. It's an investment in ourselves, and evidence that we want to wake up and effect change.

If getting out of bed is difficult for you and you regularly sleep through your alarm continually hitting the snooze button, then your vision of the future is not strong enough yet to sufficiently excite you. You need to envision more or find a new vision entirely. Mel Robbins, author of *The 5 Second Rule*, says we have about five seconds when we wake up before chaotic and negative thoughts start crowding our head making us anxious. This five seconds of freedom is all we've got to flick out our feet and leave the warm nest behind.

The essence of energy required to get you out of bed is exactly the same essence which is going to power you through your challenge to reach your dream. This is the rocket fuel of great achievement. It's called discipline and habit.

It's hard to convince yourself that you need to get up earlier, because already your sleepy brain is giving excuses as to why it's all right to go back to sleep. The lure of your still warm bed is inviting you to knock this early morning on the head today, your mind telling you, 'I promise I'll start tomorrow.' Don't be a fucking *mañana* man, the way we live our days is the way we live our lives.

Most people these days wake up fuzzy-eyed and immediately reach for their mobile phone. Because today's phones have so much to tempt us; you've got sparkly Instagram inviting your ego to check on how many likes you've had for a picture you posted. Then there's the news headlines on your phone, Black Friday sales frightening you with scarcity – *'Don't miss your last chance to get 70% discount, offer ending soon!'* To make it harder, we've woven so many of our seemingly essential activities into our phone lives that we can always use the excuse of doing something practical – checking the weather, ordering our food shop, filling in forms. In truth many of these important pieces of life admin could happily be done on a laptop or tablet that you don't have on your bedside table.

Reaching for your mobile is a habit that can be starved simply by consciously leaving your phone by your bedroom door at night. And just so you can't shout, 'Siri, turn the fucking alarm off!' – Siri being perhaps the world's worst genie in a lamp – throw a T-shirt over your phone and you'll still hear the alarm. In the time it takes you to get up and turn it off, you'll be out of your warm nest and sufficiently awake to resist going back to bed.

Instead, throw on some sweats you've left out and make your way to your chosen exercise. What a great way to start the day, working in concert with your goal, doing something useful, rather than farting, sliding back under the covers and waking up later full of self-loathing.

Your routine should not be so oppressively spartan that you hate doing it, so don't make it too rigid, work in a little bit of flex, so it becomes your friend and you enjoy doing it! We've all read those crazy 'day in the life of' diaries of people who claim to wake up at 4 a.m., pray, run a marathon, eat raw meat and lie on a bed of nails all before 6 a.m. Don't be a dick, pick some morning rituals that suit and benefit you – and that you might actually stick to. Upgrading your life should be powerful – not punishing.

On any given morning during my sacred hour, I will meditate, have an ice bath, stretch and write my journal. In terms of order, the first thing that I do is write for twenty minutes in my journal; I express gratitude, reflect on what is good and working, and get my thoughts down on the page. I write down all my goals, what my number one priority is, and one thing I can do to help bring me closer to achieving my goal today. By writing your goals every day you are strengthening the neural pathways in your brain that will help you recognise their importance and assist you to achieve them. You are aligning your attention with your intention.

Remember, if I don't do that my mind will immediately gravitate to what I *don't* want, and that it will start digging up shit from my past is evidence of this. I do some stretching to get into my body, or go for a quick walk around the block to work up a sweat and 'up' my physiology. Then I'll do a guided Blisscipline meditation to increase my focus. Finally, I take a two-minute ice bath to really ramp my shit up.

Ice Age!

The body, if allowed to by the risk-averse mind, will be as lazy as possible and try and direct you to do exactly what you did yesterday on AUTO mode, so it can play hooky and take the day off.

The brilliant thing about an ice bath is it fucking wakes you up, gives your lazy robot brain a kick up the arse and sets your body tingling as if every pore is singing with energy! And I'm not just talking about your body, your mind is flashing with activity, those neurotransmitters working to the max, making you creative, alert and courageous for the coming day.

But why is the effect of cold water on the body so positive and so powerful? Is it because it can help heal brain trauma and improve cognition? Or is it because it increases your energy and boosts your sex drive? Not only does it strengthen your immune system, it also promotes mental dominance over your body. And the Disney version? It makes you tingle and feel alive!

According to ice pioneer Wim Hof, who has broken a staggering number of Guinness World Records – among them being the first person to climb Everest in a pair of shorts, and the only man who's ever spent two hours immersed in ice with his bare flesh – well according to him, 'when we take a really cold shower, it's like an electric shock pulsing up through our spine to the deepest part of our brain, the brain stem.'

Terrific for depression, it's scientifically proven that cold water-immersion can regulate a low vibe mood of stress and anxiety, to a sense of calm. Your heartbeat also slows right down during the rest of your day following your early-morning cold-water stint. A slower heartbeat means that your body is releasing less cortisol, the chemical the brain generates when we're feeling scared or apprehensive or stressed. Also, because your metabolic rate speeds up, you feel less sluggish and more energetic, and your blood circulation is so much more fluid and therefore adds yet further energy to your system.

Now, I'm not suggesting you should go bounding into freezing cold water without any preparation. Mention it at your next check-up or speak to your doctor or practice nurse to see if it might have benefits for you and if it's safe to proceed. Every year people get into trouble or even die from cold water shock from immersion without preparation or training, so steer clear of frozen lakes and start from home instead.

The minimum amount of time for a cold shower is thirty seconds. If it's your first time, do thirty seconds after being in a hot shower. The body's vascular system, that's posh for the circulatory system, which is made up of the heart blood and blood vessels that work together to replenish the cells of the body, can manage this no problem. So, unless you've got cardiac or other circulatory issues, this is something most of us can try.

Once you've realised that thirty seconds isn't going to kill you or turn you to ice, increase up to one minute at your leisure, then gradually work your way up to two to three minutes by the tenth day of doing this. Just thirty seconds can improve memory power, thanks to the spark of neural activity which has been activated; think what two to three minutes a day will do for you, you'll be awesome!

The cold can be leveraged to increase mental strength and power, as well as resilience to stress. After ten days' regular cold or ice bathing you begin to alter your psyche for the better, releasing a calmer more energised person within you. Inflammation is reduced on a molecular level, sleep increases as well as the generation of endorphins the feel-good chemical in the brain. It can have a great social aspect to it too. Cold-water swimming should never be attempted alone if you're a beginner and there are so many clubs and groups around the country that welcome new joiners.

The British Medical Journal reports the case of a girl in her twenties who was struggling from acute anxiety and depression and who was prescribed with a weekly programme of open-water swimming. The effects were immediate as her mood strengthened, and her anxiety and depression receded so far that she was able to come off her mood-boosting drugs.

When you climb into the freezing cold in just a bikini or a pair of budgie smugglers, your body will initially scream at you like a hysterical banshee, but this reaction is normal. Your body will settle, so long as you try and distract your mind from going over the top. However, there are a number of negative effects that you would experience if you didn't listen to your body. Among them, hypothermia, brain fog and frost bite. You have to hang around for quite a bit of time to get those, but the recommended maximum time in an ice bath is three minutes. It's also worth bearing this in mind if you're lucky enough to live by the water and get your cold-water immersion in open water. Cold-water shock leads to a tragic number of drownings each year so don't overdo it or under prepare.

I bought myself an inexpensive ice bath, and it waits for me every morning. Not only does it wake me the fuck up and massively boost my energy, mentally it puts me in a good headspace too. Ice cold water has a purifying quality that can change your mood state from anxious to calm in minutes. Here is a little science, so you don't just take it from me. Yes, it temporarily makes your balls shrink back into your body and freezes your cock so it's the size of an olive, but internally, mentally and externally it's fucking good for you.

The science

When we put our head in cold water, it triggers the mammalian reflex. This is something that happens to all mammals when they immerse themselves in water; basically, to make our breath last longer, our heartbeat instantly slows down and we become calmer. Unlike 'fight', which is about raising the testosterone level to make you stronger and more aggressive, or 'flight', which raises the cortisol to speed your escape, both of which involve an increase of heartbeat, 'freeze' slows everything right down.

So, when we climb into an ice bath, lots of good things are happening. For a start, we are focusing on how freezing we are rather than letting our thoughts run amok in a negative way. Trust me, in the cold water you won't be thinking about that email you need to send. The longest nerve in the body, known as the vagus nerve, runs from the cranium all the way down to the bottom of your spine, and is often referred to as the gut-brain superhighway. The vagus nerve manages the fight-or-flight response in difficult situations.

It's the body's brake pedal that allows the mind and body to slow down in order to counter the corrosive effects of stress. In charge of delivering messages from the main organs of the body to the brain, an example of it in action is when you're stressed and you get knots in your stomach.

When you climb into an ice bath, you're activating the vagus nerve and making it work, because it puts your body into a kind of harmless stress, so that when you have real stresses in life, the vagus nerve is better toned and attuned to deal with it, and things stress you less than they would because you've got used to being stressed in the ice!

Things to avoid doing first thing in the morning

We've explored some great morning habits to cultivate. Now let's look at some of the crap we can strip out:

- Avoid all tech – it's so easy to lose valuable time fucking around on your computer or phone. Did you really need to start your day watching a TikTok dance?
- Don't start your day with comparison; looking at other people's posts while they're on holiday as you sit under the grey northern sky is not the best way to start the day, pretty soon you'll be telling yourself that your life is shit because you don't take as many holidays as your mates. Don't think about other people's wins/milestones/bodies/incomes/relationships as you start your day – think about your own.
- Do not start answering emails and allow yourself to be dragged into the rat race before you have even woken up; this is your time, not your boss's.
- Avoid any negative self-talk before you've dived into your positive morning rituals.

Twelve Stoic rules to keep us on the right path each day

Conquer the morning, using these straightforward steps:

1. In your journal, write a list of today's goals, also reflecting on the positive and negative things of yesterday, what did you learn from them?
2. Exercise, walk, swim, anything to start waking your brain and body up. Focus on your work and what you want to achieve.
3. Only focus on what you can control, not what you can't. Don't waste time on something you have no agency over. Especially the news on TV or in the papers. Again, it is essential that the first inputs you give yourself are positive and not scaremongering, triggering anxiety and self-doubt.
4. Don't let your thoughts create imaginary problems that will make you suffer. Each time you get a negative thought, recognise it and let it go. Think of something else like a question to distract you.
5. Don't kid yourself into thinking the curveballs that head your way are anything personal, they're not, the shit hits the fan for everybody at some stage. So that these negative situations don't take hold of you, try and find the silver lining. Stoics called this *amor fati*, meaning, love your fate; what can you learn from it?
6. Look at it objectively and in doing so you will depersonalise yourself from its baggage, whether it's something shit or wonderful that you're going through.
7. Focus on one goal per day and do it justice until it's finished.

8. Don't cop out by shirking or trying to take the easy way round, it will diminish and shape your character for the worse. There is no substitution for hard work and the more we push on through a difficult path, the stronger we will be from it.
9. Ask yourself if what you're doing has a purpose. Will it benefit other people? Are you growing and developing from doing it? If you can't answer at least one of these with a positive *yes*, ditch it and do something else that is useful.
10. Be hard on yourself and be compassionate to others.
11. Remember that you might well meet people today who have no control over their emotions or mouth; allow for this and don't let them bring you down to their level. Could be a thug, a miserable colleague or even a family member. Remember that story of me and the trolls, whose shitty responses I had to brace myself for when I released that video that went viral?
12. Today is another day that you give to death. The rest of your remaining life is yours to do justice to, so don't waste it – you cannot get it back.

Don't just take my word for it

In his book, *Atomic Habits*, James Clear lists four steps to creating a good habit:

- First Law: the Cue – make it obvious.
- Second Law: the Craving – make it attractive.
- Third Law: the Response – make it easy.
- Fourth Law: the Reward – make it satisfying.

Millions of people have taken Clear's advice on how to harness habits – and along with other best-selling experts like Charles Duhigg in *The Power of Habit*, there are so many powerful methods to support you in making the habits you want instinctive, effective and delivering for you.

According to scientists, sixty per cent of our actions are conscious while the remaining forty per cent happen automatically and habitually. We are only as good as our actions so the sixty per cent of consciously made decisions and actions combine to define who we are – our identity. But our habits determine our actions. If you are overweight, it's perhaps because you haven't got decent nutrition habits, or you're not in the habit of exercising, or you've developed the habit of turning to food as comfort, distraction or celebration.

When replacing a bad habit with a good one – like reading, swimming or walking – remember that if it makes you feel good it's more likely to be absorbed into your daily routine.

Habit stacking – retaining habits and building on them

Habit stacking is when we bunch new habits to existing positive habits, so that they have a better chance of sticking because there is already a foundation there. It's a great way of frontloading your day, to build your morning habits into stacks. If new habits are going to be incorporated into your life you have to place them in your path so you won't forget; like leaving your kit by your bed and your running shoes by the front door; in that way you're already prepped to go.

Maybe it's a thing you can't touch, like an affirmation, in which case write it down on a sticky note and put it somewhere where another habit takes place in the same part of the day, like the bathroom mirror where you shave or brush your teeth. The pre-frontal cortex of your brain, where data is stored, has to create a neural pathway in order for habits to become established and for them to endure. So long as you follow the same pattern every day; four weeks is all the time your brain requires to make this an established habit and a pathway that you soon forget you're following as it has become automatic. Four weeks of positive change seems to me like a very small price to pay for that.

Exercise

1. Plan your own sacred hour. If you could create four morning habits to get your day off to an energised, positive start – what would they be?
2. What's stopping you from implementing them?
3. Which one will you start first?

Shit Smells, But it's Warm – Escaping Comfort Zones

Mind vitamin

Last week I did something I never thought I'd do; I spent the day in prison. It was in Northern Ireland. HMP Magilligan, to be precise. I was invited there by one of the governors in order to give the inmates some inspiration on how to turn their lives around. BUT, and it was a bubble-butt sized BUT, it didn't go to plan. For a start, I felt a lot of nerves going in. I wasn't sure what to expect. After all, I'd never been in jail before. Sure, I've done a few 'sleepovers' in the local nick for acting like a bell-end but that's about it. So it was all very new. I felt a good few of the unpleasant emotions: uncertainty, unfamiliarity, fear, self-doubt, crisis of confidence, nerves. But it wasn't just my feelings going haywire, the projector didn't work, which meant I couldn't do the presentation as I'd planned. I had no slides to illustrate to the lads what I meant. Then I had another fucking nightmare, my laptop didn't work. So I had no references as to how far along I was in the talk. I asked them if any of them knew what a life coach was . . . only to be met by a wall of silence made out of scars and broken noses; a thousand years of collective time behind bars. It seemed the lads had never seen anyone like me in there – a speaker, or a presenter, especially one with no fancy presentation, no notes. Come on, one of you fuckers must know! I thought desperately. But not a single hand went up. Just a load of big, scary looking dudes staring at me, and clearly not impressed. Sheesh! I had already decided they thought I was a time-wasting chancer come in to drone on about how to lead a better life.

I'm feeling those emotions again just typing this (it's mad how that happens – we can really feel the echoes of our emotions). But I must tell you this. I started. And I carried on. Sharing the shit I know and believe in passionately. And, as I went on, I could see their heads starting to lift, their postures change, their shoulders going back as they started to relax, and their eyes lighting up. And, of course, we got some smiles and laughs too (just took a while for us all to get warmed up to each other).

The energy in the room did a complete 180. It was amazing! There was even a queue of fellas waiting to shake my hand and thank me when we were done.

And to top it all off, I got a tour of the prison and ended up spending half an hour in the yard with the lads, listening to them, offering advice and telling stories. I've done a lot of talks all over the world, many for mental-health charities. But this talk felt special. Like something had been activated inside of me, I felt fulfilled, grateful, appreciative, inspired and proud.

There's no way I'd have felt those incredible positive feelings and emotions without going through the scary negative ones at the start. Without pushing through the self-doubt, the nerves and the fear, I couldn't have felt the gratitude, the inspiration and the pride.

Because the truth is, I was also prepared. Sure, the slides weren't there, my laptop was bust, but I knew the content inside out and I had practised and practised what I was going to say to the point that you could've hung me a few feet above the snapping jaws of Great Whites and it's a pretty good chance I would've still remembered the order and substance of the talk.

All of the things you're looking for are on the other side of those unpleasant emotions I had to push through. The powerful emotions you want to feel – happiness, fulfilment, pride and love are on the other side of the emotions you're avoiding. So …

Stop 'sitting on the fence'.

Stop 'waiting for the right time'.

Stop 'dipping your toe in'.

Stop 'checking out the competition'.

Do your prep and then dive into the deep end.

THAT'S HOW YOU LEARN TO SWIM!

Fear and anxiety, as well as being excellent alarm clocks, are the emotions of growth.

Disappointment and failure, when treated correctly, are also a prerequisite for success. Ex SAS specialist, Jay Morton, believes that fear is a growth space and that we should breathe in the fear and see it as a good thing. Conor McGregor, MMA fighter, is known for saying, 'there is only winning and learning'. The law of polarity states that there is no pain without gain, or no gain without pain. So, in order to extract yourself from being trapped in a gilded cage, you're going to have to push yourself into the unknown as that is where the juicy kick-ass things happen. Just remember Chris Lewis as a good example of this, brothers and sisters. It's time to leave your comfort zones.

There is a saying in Alcoholics Anonymous, *'Shit smells but it's warm.'* In other words, most of us are prepared to tolerate a situation that is bad for us (smells), but at least we know where we are (the warmth of familiarity), rather than bravely exposing ourselves to the unknown. What we don't seem to realise is that positive change only happens when there's a space where something has moved out of the way to allow the new thing to happen. Our brain hates surprises and will try its best not to allow change in, and no matter how unhealthy a situation might have become – be it a toxic relationship, a job that dulls our soul, or us shooting-up in a cold-water squat – unless this current situation is immediately physically threatening us, the lazy computer in our brain tells us to tolerate it; after all we are just repeating a pattern we've already shown hasn't killed us, the primitive brain has no reason to make us change. This is how so many of us live, at a base level of existence, without real freedom and happiness, not daring to dream that over the brow of the next hill is something/someone better suited to who we are. If only we could trust the unknown. Trust the journey.

Sometimes our lazy brain computer isn't just saving energy and allowing/supporting us to remain in stagnant situations that under-nourish our imagination and spirit; sometimes it actively overreacts in order to resist change, using our fight-or-flight mechanism. This is why when you start to challenge your comfort-zone-loving brain it will most likely push back with an over-dramatic worst-case scenario. The following are a few examples of its pushbacks.

The toxic relationship

'Okay, so she loses her temper, makes me feel like a piece of excrement and puts me down in front of my friends. *But* the sex is good after an argument. And so what if she flirts with other men, it's me she leaves the club with (most of the time) at the end of the night. Maybe things will return to being like they used to be at the start of our relationship, when we respected each other. And it's better than being alone. I might never find someone else to love me.'

A job that dulls the soul

'Imagine how scary it will be if you don't have this job! How will you feed the kids and pay the mortgage? And what makes you think you've got the minerals to leave here? At least you know how to do this job standing on your head. How would you learn something new? How would you get through an interview or start up on your own? You've only got another twelve years here and then you'll be retiring. Play it safe.'

Cold-water flat

'Okay, so there's mould all over the ceiling and the bairn has a bad cold. But it's better than nothing and nobody knows you're here, no police or social services looking for us. And you can score gear off the landlord too. Things could be worse, at least you've got your crack and you're dry in here.'

Dr Joe Dispenza has this to say on comfort zones: 'Human nature is such that we resist changing until things get really bad and we're so uncomfortable that we can no longer go on with business as usual. This is as true for an individual as it is for a society. We wait for crisis, trauma, loss, disease and tragedy before we get down to looking at who we are, what we're doing, how we're living, what we're feeling, and what we believe or know in order to embrace true change.'

We humans constantly talk ourselves out of rich opportunities in favour of the bland, predictable and soul-destroying routine we are stuck in. This is how people end up in a prison of their own making, doing the same old shitty job for thirty years and then picking up a gold watch at the end? I don't think there's even a fucking gold watch these days. We live for Fridays in quiet desperation, only for Saturday to be over too quick and the same old hamster-wheel shit starts again every Monday, and surprise, surprise, we feel as if we are slowly drowning.

The greatest regret

Being stuck on the treadmill of predictability is doing what you have always done. If you're sleepwalking deeply enough through life, there's a pretty good chance you might only wake up on your deathbed and get a bit of clarity. As we mentioned at the start, often people just about to take their last breath realise that they played their life too safe, and that they could've taken a few big risks and still survived, had things gone south.

But not everybody gets to live their life in quiet comfort zones, some of us lucky ones get curveballed, dragged down, knocked over – have our life turned upside down. And yes, we really are the lucky ones, because when we fall to absolute zero, we can't fall any lower or feel any worse, and the only options open to us are roll over and die. Or, decide that's not an option and that it's time to climb out of the hole and start to rebuild our lives and make the most of them before we are too decrepit to be able to make any meaningful change.

Things happen for a reason

We've all seen or heard that preface 'I'm willing to bet …' – either said to us apologetically when we've faced some shock or trauma, or meant as a comfort when some apparently meaningless tragedy hits. And while it's easy to brush that line off, you don't have to be religious or superstitious to find the truth in it.

Things *don't* often happen randomly in life, almost all events come from cause and effect. It might be a cause you can't control, but if you look at the circumstances, there's almost always a cause there – they occur for a reason. Which means there's usually also an opportunity attached if you can only find it.

When your marriage breaks down – maybe your wife cheats on you, maybe you cheat on your wife – that's because you have lost your connection with them, and one of you feels sufficiently empty/sad/reckless to do something as extreme as having an affair. It's often exposing an unhealthy marriage, and the split is a chance to either fix it or move on and fix yourself. Or it might result in one of you leaving and finding another partner. Getting through the dark days leads to self-discovery, and it can also need to new love on the other side of disappointment.

Perhaps the reason you got sacked from that job you hated was because it was clear (to everyone but you sometimes) that your heart wasn't in it, and this is what you need to force you into taking a chance on starting your own business now, before it is too late and someone else comes up with your brilliant idea. Something must shift, must direct us into unknown territory to be able to push through. It's in the 'I don't know' when the fun starts. And what it takes is courage to let go of what you know and that's no longer making you grow and trusting that something better will take its place.

The reasons aren't always clear when you're going through it all, but you can almost always see them as you look back, so trust in that as you keep moving forward.

Terrible things, seemingly random accidents can even be rich in purpose. You wouldn't wish them to happen but if they do, you can find purpose in them. Take Roberto Durán, the famous Panamanian boxer, who fought professionally for over three decades, long after his contemporaries like Marvin Hagler and Sugar Ray Leonard had hung up their gloves and retired. The only thing that could stop him was a severe car accident that made it impossible for him to box again. You have to ask yourself whether this was sweet destiny intervening.

I believe that mental breakdowns happen in order to teach us something of vital importance. They are one of the body's alarm clocks and can act as a handbrake and force us to violently stop, often in dramatic fashion. Like any emergency stop, they're not comfortable, and where you can, it's better to stop gently before your body or mind slams on the brakes. But if that's the only way you can stop, then it's still a much-needed halt. It may just be our inner wisdom, which, having tried to convince us earlier that we were going down the wrong route, is now forced to take us to the dark place because that's the only way that it can force a change which is really needed. In layman's terms, bad shit that happens to us pushes us somewhere better – towards a different goal, relationship, opportunity, country, job or fresh path.

Tyson Fury's wake-up call came when he was aiming his fine new Ferrari at an oncoming bridge in order to end his life; pulling away from it seconds before impact because he realised he didn't want to do this to his children. He had to go that low and that close to the edge in order to find his meaning and purpose, which is being a dad as well as a fighter. I wouldn't wish anyone there, or with me on that ledge in South Shields, but know that if that is where you find yourself, there's a different path to turn to, even at the last chance.

If your purpose is not the right purpose, your inner wisdom will keep making you fall off that wagon, until you accept you are going the wrong way. Like an actor who after ten years of sweat, tears and little success to show for it, realises he might be better off focusing his efforts on his other skill as a writer. As soon as he stops acting and holding on desperately to something that's never going to happen, the writing opportunities start flooding in. Where our true purpose and intention goes, focus flows. Just remember, you can't beat reality but you can listen to it and realise it's not all doom-mongering. A 'no' to one thing is often truly a 'yes' to something else. So, are we really falling off the wagon or are we unconsciously choosing to do something that's not in line with who we thought we would be?

Accept yourself

I believe that it's never a fall if we shouldn't have been on that wagon in the first place (yes, we're back to my words about authentic and passionate purpose again). If your wagon isn't heading in the right direction, falling off is a blessing in disguise. At forty-two, I finally stopped fighting who I am. I've found peace because I've accepted my insecurities and I've owned my imperfections. When I fall off the mood wagon it's because I've got low mood energy and I'm forgetting about the excitement of the future and where I want to be. To address this I just go to my purpose and goals and realign with them.

Comfort zones are not comfortable

So in truth, a comfort zone is not a comfort zone for very long. Staying still can feel like a much-needed rest at first, but soon we'll start to feel stagnant. A human being is the greatest contradiction, because while we may be wired to avoid danger and our brains prefer to keep us safe by being lazy, a big part of us is also designed to respond positively to challenges and to want to discover new things. Change is life. It's why challenge, innovation and discovery are also hardwired into us – they just lurk beneath the bit of the brain that wants to wrap us and keep us comfortable. The pyramids of Egypt wouldn't have been built without the impossible ambition of mankind, neither would the Golden Gate Bridge (at the time everybody laughed at the guy who built it and said it wasn't possible). Humans have a side to us which is amazing, it's the dream builder.

Everything you have ever wanted is just outside your comfort zone, unless of course you want to feel static, unambitious and stale. If you avoid the discomfort of exercise you end up with the discomfort of being fat and lacklustre, the law of polarity dictates this. Someone in a relationship who avoids the discomfort of having an honest conversation with their partner will end up with the more painful discomfort of a break-up on their hands further down the line. No pain, no gain. You don't grow muscles by looking at weights, you have to pump iron to force muscular growth.

If I don't seek out discomforts that inspire me, I will attract discomfort that drains the life out of me. This is at the heart of Upgrading. This way, it is me who gets to choose my level of discomfort. Life should be a growth-centric experience. We need to embrace change in order to soak up all the colours that our existence has to offer. I recently signed up to walk to Everest base camp. Now, that might seem like an extremely daft thing to do, and the obvious discomfort my thighs and calves are going to get at that gradient, not forgetting altitude sickness and the possibility I might have to come straight down the mountain if I start showing the symptoms, but the discomfort is what it's all about. Because for all the physical pain, preparation, effort and expense of the trip, there is a lifelong memory of seeing the world's highest mountain. You can't put a price on that. I'm so excited because it's a challenge with such a fantastic reward and just thinking about it, makes my present that much more exciting with the anticipation of the future.

Relationships

A lot of people stay in dysfunctional relationships because they are scared to be on their own, or because they've been with the other person for as long as they can remember and it's become a habit; there is little to no love or connection in their relationship; no creativity, and nothing grows – but fear can be (almost) as powerful as love. Sure, there are couples where one has an affair to escape the boredom, but most people, even in failing relationships, will not take the risk and so end up together until it's too late to either mend or change it. You might not have put me down as a poetry fan, but W.H. Auden once wrote, 'The desert sighs in the bedroom, the glacier creaks in the bed, a crack in the teacup opens, a lane to the land of the dead.'

The danger of staying in a lifeless relationship is that your opposite partner may well leave you anyway. I'm not saying you should get out first – not at all – but you can be the proactive person who starts the conversation to wake you both up, whether that's to improvement or a bigger decision. It's time to ask yourself what you're bringing to the table. When we look at cracks in relationships, we often look outward rather than inward. One of the biggest challenges in a relationship is when one (or both sides) of the partnership don't like themselves, and so rely on their other half for affirmation. Your partner isn't there to fill a void in you. They're there to support you in your life as you support them. If one partner is looking for all their energy and validation from the other it's easy to become needy and the relationship is unbalanced. It's a breeding ground for resentment if you're waiting for the other person to be your energy. Relationships are like a see-saw and you give and receive support at different times but if you're lucky and you're with the right person and circumstances are in your favour, there's a Goldilocks zone, an equilibrium where each person is in love with the other and does things to show this. There is equal trust and faith in the relationship, where neither person takes the other for granted.

But then as is so often the case, one day shit happens and knocks one person's self-confidence off balance, so that they require more TLC than usual. A good relationship allows you to verbalise this need and communicate with each other, like telling your other half you feel fed up and you need a hug. If you're in the right relationship with the right person they naturally know what to do to make you feel stronger again. And a great relationship means the other person also has times where they can ask for and receive support – in their own way. It shouldn't be a one-way street. And when it's not working? It's not necessarily about asking for support and not getting it. A bad relationship doesn't allow you to ask, for fear of seeming weak or needy. In the old days, before I was comfortable asking my wife for attention, I would go off on a three-day bender, self-soothing with drugs and booze because I didn't know how to communicate, if I could, or what I was even asking for.

Now, I know when I've got an issue that I need to work on myself and when the problem is one that Mrs Mort can help with. I went to watch a boxing match recently and I was so adrenalised by it (must be the Viking bloodlust of my ancestors coming out!) that I couldn't sleep for love nor money afterwards and I was still awake at 4.30 a.m. The next day I was in pieces, having only had a few hours' sleep. This was on top of missing a lot of sleep in the same period with a pec injury. Anyway, I told my wife I needed a little bit of TLC, and she gladly gave it. Many of us don't know how to ask for warmth, so we end up 'acting up' as a way of getting attention. A relationship in balance isn't only about asking for help with the things we can't solve ourselves, it's allowing the other person to comfort and support us in ways that nourish them as well as ourselves. You don't make a brew for your partner only when they're too busy or stressed to get one themselves – you do it naturally, and the same should be true of the bigger gestures too.

How to move on from a relationship

Not all relationships are healable. It's not to say they were always wrong, but some relationships – romantic, professional or platonic – work only for a period of our lives. How do you move through them without damaging yourself or the other partner?

Upgrade fact: you can't move on from anything that you can't say 'thank you' for

Even when something's run its course, you don't need to be bitter. If you can leave with positivity, both sides will heal faster. If you can't be grateful for it (whether that's for the good parts, or whether it's simply for it being over) then it's harder to consign it to the past. Instead, it will become emotional baggage that will weigh you down and spread negativity into the rest of your life.

You need to find five positives for the relationship being over, in order that in six months' time you can look back at it and say, 'Thank God, we moved on from that at the right time.' Right now, if you're leaving a relationship or you've just left one, it's probably fucking hard to identify *any* positives because it's all still emotional and raw. One cathartic thing we can do to help cut through all that emotional fog is journalling, getting how we feel down onto the page. By writing about the past, you are able to understand what went wrong, then leave it there on the page rather than in your mind. Journalling is also a great way of recognising and validating emotions, then letting them go as you turn the page. It's fine to be sad, but then you can leave that emotion behind once it's done its work.

Ultimately, we each need to work on our relationship with ourselves, because if that is fucked we have no stable basis from which to give love to another person. No one else can complete us, only us. Happiness and self-worth must come from within us and not rely on other people. When you pay attention to yourself and what you are good at you become grateful. When you focus on what you are doing well and what you like about yourself, you begin to change the energy, shifting it to a place where you are ready to ask for and receive abundance. Relationships are so much easier when your self-worth is high. Upgrading your relationships always starts with upgrading your relationship with you.

I get a lot of, 'Paul, I hate myself, how do I love myself?'

I ask them, 'How do you treat someone that you love?'

'I do nice things for them, like reassure them when they are low, tell them how I feel about them, feed them healthy food …'

I tell them, 'This is how you need to start treating yourself. Maybe take yourself off to the movies or go for a massage.' I also add, 'Notice what you say to someone you love.' If you compliment them on how they look, or how well they are doing, their self-worth goes up. When there is a conflict of values relationships often don't work.

Bruce Lee once said, 'Don't speak negatively about yourself even as a joke. Your body doesn't know the difference. Words are energy and cast spells, that's why it's called spelling. Change the way you speak about yourself, and you can change your life. What you're not changing, you're also choosing.'

We need to make sure that we are constantly feeding our unconscious with encouraging thoughts to raise our self-worth, which will in turn enhance our ability to visualise positively.

I had a client who had been with his girlfriend since they were teenagers. Sadly, she left him for someone else. She was the love of his life and he was gutted. So why, you may ask, would he be grateful for splitting up with her? Well, for a start it was better to find out what she was up to then rather than wasting more years only to find out further down the line that she didn't share the same values or feelings. He now had more time to himself so he could invest in a little bit of self-love; he could travel more, focus on his business more and yes, eventually, meet other women.

By being thankful for leaving a bad relationship, you neutralise it so it doesn't become something that you resent, because that will only rob you of positive energy. As ever, to truly move on we need to have something to head towards, something that excites us about the future. Ask yourself where you would like to travel to, who you want to hang out with, what you would like to talk about with them, how you would like to feel. Remember, if you want to make your present better you need to make your future bigger. The bigger something is, the more gravitational pull it asserts. Be grateful for what's passed and now shift the focus to the future.

Enjoying your own company

As well as learning to be positive about yourself, and not finding your validation in other people, creating happiness from within yourself means you won't waste time and money searching for it externally. You might think Upgrading means buying the newest, best and priciest version of everything out there. But however much you think having a top of the range Porsche might just be the best thing in the world for you, it's not going to make you happy. No, that starts with your inner self, being your best coach and learning what makes you tick. As well as being a way of releasing and moving on from negative emotions, journalling is a great way of capturing and recording the positives because you get to know your thoughts as you put them on paper. I call my journal 'The Inventory of Awesomeness' and I use it to pick out things in the day that I'm grateful for.

When I first got into personal development in 2006, I listened to all the quotes about negative people and how I needed to make sure I wasn't surrounded by them. 'At all costs avoid mood hoovers and energy vampires.' I thought that was all I needed to do. But being isolated after I'd done that showed me that shutting myself off from other people was no use if I couldn't rely on myself to fill that space.

Some people don't know any different than to complain, it's as if it has been bred into them. My mum is a champion gossip and whinger. She knows it too. She's never given me any praise whatsoever. She's never really told me that she loves me, although her actions do prove it beyond any shadow of a doubt. If she didn't gossip about other people, my mum and I would have nothing to talk about. It used to get on my nerves, and I'd try and avoid her: the energy vampire! Bless her. But one day my nan was round at hers at the same time I was, and to my surprise I heard my mum bigging me up to my nana, saying, 'You'll never guess what car Paul's just bought.' *God*, I thought, *finally me mam is saying something positive about me. That's a first!*

Then my nan turned to me and said, 'Did you know your mum went to grammar school and got all these qualifications and she just ended up working in a bar.'

At that moment, I perfectly understood why Mum was as she was, she knew no different; she'd been taught to be that way by my nan.

We need to remember that we're all trying our best with the tools we've got. For some people, being negative is the only way that they can feel better. Complaining at some level is probably therapeutic for some people. They've never been shown an alternative way to be, and doubtless they've grown up around complainers. I get a lot of shit on the internet, people trolling and trying to pull me down. The sad thing about trolls is you have to be pretty desperate and feel very shit about yourself, to get your kicks from being mean about someone else. You've got to feel sorry for them really. They live life in an exaggerated version of a place we can probably all recognise. Find me a person that never complains and I'll walk around Asda naked for two hours. Most of us have a bit of a moan now and then – but ask yourself if it's becoming a habit and taking over the majority of your interactions. And look at your outlets, purposes and actions. Most of us complain mentally and not verbally, which can be fine – as long as you know why you're doing it. Is it just a vent, a thought that needs thinking then you're done with it? Or is the whinge a call to action or a drive to change that you're ignoring. If you can find the grit that's causing it, you can do something about it. Unless, of course, you just like moaning.

Remember, there's a difference between legitimate complaint, emotional expression and just good old-fashioned whingeing. It's dangerous to mistake them for each other – so don't shut it down until you can work out what that voice really is. Then do something about it!

Comfort zones in business

If you avoid discomfort to grow your company, you stay in the same place or you go out of business. When you make the decision to stay where you are and not grow, it means you're not evolving, and when people realise they're working for a company that is not progressing they tend to leave. When you evolve, you gather momentum and people want to be a part of that trajectory. We all want to be involved in a success story not a slowly sinking ship. The way to evolve and pull yourself out of comfort zones is to set new goals and new targets, creating a compelling view of the future, then sharing it with your staff so they become a part of it.

Exercise

1. Look back at the last three years and pick three things that seemed tough at the time but in hindsight you can see the opportunity they brought or the lesson they taught.
2. Write down one thing that someone you admire does that you would like to do if only you had the confidence. Then write down what the first step to achieving that goal would be.

Finding Your Wolfpack – Like-Minded People

Mind vitamin

Finding the right peer group is no cinch, and you have to really look for it. And leaving the one you may currently be in or making changes to yourself while you're still in it is hard. Your peers might say, 'Why you not drinking?' Or 'Just have one.' Or 'I wouldn't do that if I were you.' Or 'Don't do that …' But the journey is worth it.

In 2014, I was given the opportunity to attend a training course that I thought could change my life. It wasn't easy to get to. But its value has been immense. I was among a group of men who were just like me; they had a passion for levelling up, trying to do and be better, who got excited about the future. And in those five days a new life transpired for me.

The mistake people make when they finally understand how important it is to align themselves to the right people to propel themselves forward, is that often they're not prepared to look beyond their back garden. If you were looking for your romantic soulmate you'd probably make a bit more effort than going to your local pub to meet 'the one'– you might need to travel further afield.

I remember when I used to run workshops in Newcastle, people used to say, 'Can you not run one in Manchester, please?'

'For fuck's sake!' I said. 'It's only two hours' drive to Newcastle!'

You have to get up off your arse if you want meaningful change in your life, and you've got to be hungry for it and be prepared to travel to find it; nothing is achieved alone in your front room. The journey might begin there – but it likely won't end there. You're probably going to have to leave your town or country to find the right wolfpack but once you've found it it'll be worth it. I've certainly had to travel the world to find my wolfpack and I didn't find it immediately. It's taken me quite a long time and a lot of air miles, but it was worth the wait.

A really tight wolfpack is one in which a bunch of like-minded people understand, support and motivate each other, and they all operate on a similar frequency. I have a jujitsu club right on my doorstep, which is great for some people, however, I choose to go to another one which is half an hour's drive away. Why? Because it's a better fit for me – it's of a higher standard and they expect more of me there, which means I have to show up with my best self. When you're around people who want to level up and improve, there's nothing quite like it, it's a rare energy and all you can do is get better by being around them.

Where is your wolfpack? Remember, it won't come to you, you have to find it.

Tony Robbins says, 'The results that you have in your life are in direct correlation to the standards that your peer group hold you to.' If you want to do better, you have to share the company of people with higher standards. It's inbuilt into human nature that we want to be accepted, we want the rewards we get from being social animals. This behaviour goes back millennia to our hunter-gatherer days when we lived in caves and sought the protection of a tribe, and later when we started to form communities. When we were upright hominids we became increasingly social animals out of necessity, in order to bring down bigger prey like mammoths we needed to work together. So the group could sleep safely, someone had to be on watch, someone had to tend the fire to keep the predators at bay ... all these acts were socially cohesive, we were the hominid massive! As recently as 15,000 years ago we were still being hunted by hairy mammals with big teeth. A part of us, even now, is worried about being forced out of the cave.

So group dynamics are powerful and deep-rooted. Peer pressure, when those around us require us to change to meet the standards of the group, is usually thought of as negative – but remember it can run both ways. It may be that to fit in you feel you have to put weight on, or dumb down. Or it may be that you have to raise your game in order to be equal to them. The worst of peer pressure is bullying, the best is inspiration – and the very best, is when that inspiration comes not from your peers, but from yourself, because of your peers.

In jujitsu, if you just roll with white belts you may feel pleased with yourself, but you'll never get better. The only way up is to train with people who are better than you. In areas of my life where I want to get better, I seek out the appropriate peer groups. Make sure you get a seat on the table where people are talking actively about their future, not one where they are just complaining about everybody else. It's about finding a group with the right energy to lift you and help you be the best version of you. I love being around people who tell me the story of their future rather than talking about their past. I also like to seek out others who are further ahead than me on the same path, that way I can learn from their mistakes and save myself a lot of time. When I first moved to Harrogate in the year 2000, I'd never really seen different definitions of success; my dad worked in a factory and my mum worked at Asda. They worked incredibly hard, but I realised early on that employed life wasn't for me. Nobody in my family was self-employed. But in Harrogate I started meeting people with a little bit of money, and being out of my childhood environment I realised that there are actually people who are successful who are not evil and aren't ripping people off. And when I interview people for my podcast who are doing amazing things, I often think, they are not that different to me, and if they can do it, so can I. It's like a little bit of magic dust rubs off on me. My big might be their normal, but being given that exposure gives me the belief that with time and energy, discipline and focus, I can catch them up. It's not enough to see great people – you have to see the stepping stones that go from you to them. And they are there, trust me.

Having people around you who've got your back, who encourage and give you support when you need it, is essential to leading a happy life. We're not designed to be on our own for too long. Human beings have climbed to the top of the food chain because of their ability to band together and collaborate. We are at our strongest when we are connected to a group we trust and feel a part of.

There are certain people who will knock your confidence (often by accident) by questioning your ability, or keeping you in an old identity that you've moved on from. Some friends will feel threatened by the new you and your success, others will drain you with their neediness but never offer the support when you need their help. It's important to find the right people who are resonating on the same frequency. There are plenty of people out there who'll inspire you or spur you on when you're at a low ebb. Sharing the same values and a common interest is the cement that forms new relationships. I found my tribe through jujitsu.

Criteria for finding the right wolfpack:

- Are the people in this group moving in the same direction as me?
- Are there some people that are already where I want to be?

- Is this group of people excited about their future?
- What's the 'price' (time, effort, money, etc) I need to pay to be a part of it?
- Will I need to raise my standards to play the game with these people?
- Does the group have a proven track record of the kind of results I'm looking for?

Back in 2001, when I was just starting out as a coach and a training entrepreneur, I studied a course called 'Get the Edge' with Tony Robbins. It was so long ago that he was on QVC, the shopping channel, and they sent you a DVD or a CD boxset. One of the first things Robbins said, and this really stuck with me, was that: 'The results you have in your life are a direct correlation to the standards that your peer group holds you to.'

It didn't make sense to me until years later when I was participating in the training course I've mentioned – 'Wake Up Warrior'. It was 2014 and I was at my lowest ebb. I was put in a group with a bunch of men who were all very ambitious, driven characters, and without exception all were further ahead on the path of success than me in terms of their health, their energy, and business. By being among them I suddenly started feeling that I wanted to raise the bar of my own standards to the levels that they had achieved. And the great thing was they held me to account if I didn't do what I said I was going to do. We would meet every quarter to have a planning session, where we would declare our intentions for the next three months, so everybody on the course knew exactly what to expect in terms of progress from each individual the next time that we met.

There was a pro American footballer on the course, he had already won the Super Bowl, and he was the first person to challenge me and say, 'You said you'd do that last time. Why haven't you done it?' *At last*, I thought, *somebody is calling me out on my bullshit.*

I started to see the power of being among people who are motivated and moving in the same direction as me. Like it or not we are all subject to the 'law of conformity', the process whereby people change their behaviour, appearance or their attitudes, to better fit in to a group. It's been suggested that there are three types of conformity:

- Compliance: the weakest form of the three, when a person changes their ways and appearance to fit in with that of the group. Privately, however, they may not agree with the group.
- Identification: when a person is drawn to a group because of their values or something that the group represents.
- Internalisation: the strongest form of conformity, because it involves accepting the norms and beliefs of the group in private and publicly.

We tend to modify our behaviour to fit in with the peer group we are in at any one time. You will either lower or raise your standards in order to fit in with a peer group, but you can be in several peer groups at the same time. In 2014, of all the mates I was hanging out with, I was the most financially successful. But I knew I was a mess on other fronts, part of why I went on the Warrior course. I knew I needed some other peer groups.

If you're not surrounded by people who are in line with who you are trying to become it's harder for you. If the people in your environment – remember, environment always trumps willpower. If their beliefs and behaviours are in direct competition with the way you want to behave and progress, then you're left with willpower alone because your environment is not right.

You don't need to remove anybody from your life, none of that dramatic bullshit, just find a group of people – whether that's online or in person – who you relate to. It really can be a case of different people for different situations, different needs. I now have a network of people who I can call upon to help with a number of things. In return I ask them how I can be useful, what's in my skill set that they haven't got which I can help with.

In the UK alone, the suicide rate in men between forty and fifty is 5,000 per year. It's an epidemic, and the reason it is happening is because many men don't have the language to discuss their mindset nor a mission that inspires them, so they feel lost and disenfranchised. They have no set of shared beliefs that bind them to others. When I was lost, I needed a group and I found this through my new jujitsu brothers.

Jujitsu worked for me because I'd found out enough about myself to know that **variety** was key for me so I never got bored.

Work out what your key is (it might be creativity or being outdoors or being structured) – and then you'll see the other benefits that flow from that. Some of mine were:

- Challenge: I was constantly learning, which kept my mind busy.
- Fitness: jujitsu kept my body fit and after I slept better and rested better.
- Structure: it gave me routine as I knew I'd be training on set nights of the week so I had to plan better.
- Comrades: it gave me a sense of brotherhood that I knew was reciprocated – people were waiting on me to show up.
- Risk: it had an element of danger which I really need to focus my energy on – I have to concentrate, otherwise I get the shit beaten out of me.

Finding your wolfpack is one of the fastest ways to Upgrade your life. But it requires attention. You have to water your relationships. It's a small regular practice that supercharges your friendships. A couple of minutes of checking in with people will change your life. As you get older you tend to have less disposable time, you need to use it carefully as it's precious, but that also means it's more appreciated when you give it to the network of people around you. Like so many things in life, it's quality not quantity. An hour spent sitting in a pub on your phone next to one of your mates is not going to give either of you as much as a fifteen-minute call on your way to work to ask how they're really doing. Sometimes it's smaller still – a joke, a message or check-in to say you've remembered the stress they're going through will build your wolfpack bonds.

Exercise

On a scale of one to ten, how aligned with your future is your current peer group and what is in the gap between the two?

Shut the Fuck Up – Understanding Anxiety

Mind vitamin

In 2016, I was flying to a friend's wedding in Syracuse. New York from Newcastle, via Heathrow and Chicago. On the way there I could feel a panic attack taking hold. I was on one of the flights. Suddenly I wanted to speak to my kids, who back then were three and six years old. I started picturing them saying, 'When's Dad going to be home?' The overwhelming feeling that I'm on my own, trapped on the plane, gives me the sweats and my heart starts jackhammering against my chest. The stewardess rang the doctor, then she opened a suitcase and gave me a diazepam. That calmed me a little for the rest of the flight. But was it the answer? Soon I was off that plane and waiting in Chicago for the next flight to New York. I had another panic attack and missed my flight.

When it passed (and they do pass – always remember that) I recalled that I had recently attended a retreat where they teach you how to deal with panic attacks. Of course, I'd not been able to think at all in the middle of the panic attack, but I knew I could use their toolkit now. The retreat had shown how panic attacks and anxiety could be lessened or even avoided by diverting your attention or talking to someone in order to distract yourself. So, I downloaded Angry Birds *on my phone and on the next flight completely immersed myself in that and before I knew it we had arrived in Syracuse. 'Paul,' you'll say, 'I thought you were all about leaving your phone behind?' But it was just the bridge I needed. After one successful flight I could tell a different story to myself. Since then I've never needed medication for any form of anxiety. Don't worry, I'm not playing* Angry Birds *every time I get on board.*

Of course, if you've experienced 'generalised anxiety', as it's often labelled, the very name suggests it's not one thing that triggers it. Previously going to the dentist was a major trauma for me, but using this technique of self-distraction I could tackle that too. I was hardly going to be able to be on my phone while in the chair so instead I said to the dentist, 'I get a bit overwhelmed at the dentist, I'd like you to talk to me all the way through this procedure please.' After losing my two front teeth boxing, it was a huge bit of surgery I was having – he was putting a plate into my gum. He talked to me all the way through the procedure and I made sure I listened and placed my attention purely on him. It worked a treat! And all because I'd been able to ask rather than pretend I was fine.

Realising I have the power to direct my thoughts towards what I want, and not what I don't, is one of the most life-changing lessons I've ever learnt. When we're feeling empowered we can redirect our own thoughts – but if anxiety strikes, then using props and other people to help achieve that goal is a great route through.

Everyone's experience of anxiety will be different but here's what has worked and continues to work for me.

When it comes to research, the one source I avoid is Dr Google. I found I was feeding rather than calming my anxiety by endlessly googling. Over-analysing can cause anxiety as much if not more than it can alleviate it. For me, anxiety is not a mental illness, it's a bodily function, a physiological response to fear. Whether that fear is real or proportionate is the key.

Anxiety can be life altering. It comes in many different forms like phobias, PTSD, OCD, panic attacks and social anxiety. There are a wealth of different therapies and treatments you can try. But I've found so many people on my courses have never needed to read any more about anxiety after I've taught them what I learnt.

I was not the typical anxious type, biting my nails and looking nervous. What I had were panic attacks. It was like a pile-on at school, where everybody jumps on you and you can't get out. That was what my first panic attack felt like – a physical attack. There were many more afterwards. Once I had one in Marbella where I got stuck in a hotel room because the lock was stuck. I had another in a hotel toilet in Thailand. Not surprisingly, I now dislike hotel toilets immensely and have to take a shit with the lock off using my foot to stop anyone trying to get in! In short, I could write the book on panic attacks. But hopefully after this chapter, neither you nor I will need that.

Don't let anxiety be the story

Anxiety is not an illness, you can't catch it. It's a response to disordered fear. Fear is a rational emotion, anxiety is not, it is a state, and it has its own characteristic physiology: short breath, increased temperature, higher heart rate. Fear or nerves often come with a distinct cause and awareness. Anxiety often comes unconsciously. And it will feed on attention and grow to fill the space you give it. If you label yourself as someone who has anxiety it's often a self-fulfilling prophecy, and you will keep having it. What your mind is actually doing is making inappropriate risk assessments, trying to keep you safe by hitting the big red panic button without proportionate cause. Anxiety is not logical. We know we're not going to die of our panic attack, but we are letting the amygdala, our fear response centre in the brain, create an unnecessarily dramatic response. That's why panic attacks can feel so crushing – the fear comes from the same place in your brain as 'rational' fear – of a genuine life threat, palpable danger or fight-or-flight scenario. We just need to start reprogramming our unconscious mind so it can tell the amygdala to stand down.

What doesn't work

For me, counselling, psychology and psychotherapy don't work for my panic attacks. Why? Because it's bringing anxiety to the front of my conscious mind. The thing that is making you anxious, you are talking about it, foregrounding it. Maybe you'll feel a little bit better in the session, but your anxiety won't go away. You can't remove inappropriate fear responses by focusing on them. You have to remove and replace anxiety with a different focus, right?

I've tried other approaches too. It's the same with the mood diary, it doesn't work for me. Keeping an anxiety diary means you're constantly focusing on something that you're trying to get rid of. It's not going to remove it. Anxiety is a subconscious thing that lives in the basement. It's made up of our neural pathways. Giving myself time to sit with it achieves nothing for me. It's like when you break your leg and it's in a cast and then it heals. Do you keep the cast on, or do you take it off and learn how to walk again? You don't focus on the fact it was broken you just move forward and get on with things. I find that by constantly talking about it you're watching the weeds instead of uprooting them so they die.

And while I was grateful for that diazepam the air hostess gave me, I didn't want a lifetime of anti-anxiety medication. I knew that with my brain chemistry, pills can't make me fearless. Anxiety is a disordered fear response, so by taking a pill you don't get rid of fear, even if you feel it less. It's a subconscious autonomic response rather than a disease.

Anxiety will trample over the things we used to love, if we let it

Socialising.
Work.
Time with friends & family.
Learning and training.
Hobbies.
Goals.
Ambitions.

If you look at that list and recognise lots of those things, you'll see you have a lot going on, a pretty full life. You have what we might call a divergent focus – lots of things you're interested in. So how do you go from that to an anxious person?

Maybe something happens in your social life and you don't feel great meeting up with people after this incident. Or maybe something happens at work that really upset you. Perhaps something happened on a plane like bad turbulence. Whatever it is that you used to do, you've now stopped doing it after having experienced that fear response because you don't want the fear and panic to happen again.

As we get older, our lives have a tendency to shrink. Our friendship base dwindles and we meet up with mates less often. We no longer have as many hobbies as we used to and gradually, very incrementally, our focus begins to narrow. So, as we socialise less it feels like we're working more. Maybe we get around to seeing our family occasionally, and still do a bit of exercise. But we've gone from having a busy varied life, one in which our brains were focused on divergent activities, to one where we do less, even if we focus on what we do do more intensely. I have long felt this is why there was so much anxiety during the pandemic – apart from the frontline workers, there was too much space for most of us to fill, and a little overwhelmed by it, instead of using the time to do more to feed our brains, we ended up doing far less; working, but staying at home to do it, with maybe a half-hour walk during the day, in which we saw no one; gravitating towards Netflix – or Facebook or Instagram, where we looked at other people living *better* lives, being in *better* places than we were! Poor us!

So with a focus that's now really narrow, and really self-oriented, what sits in the gap between a fulfilled life and a life that's become smaller? Copious amounts of extra room which leaves ample space for anxiety, worry and panic attacks to fill that vacuum.

The time in my life where I suffered the most anxiety was when I was in Spain and I had stopped setting goals or seeing people. I wasn't pushing myself or exercising. I thought I wanted an easy life, so I stopped going to events, stopped learning or growing. I was left with two things: my family and some business stuff, but I had set even those up to have minimal touchpoints. My life became very small. I had a lot of hunger intellectually as I wasn't challenging my mind. Instead, my mind used its time and space and energy to feel small problems were big, life-threatening ones, and inappropriate responses to fear. I'm lucky to have a creative brain – but if I don't use it, when my life isn't full, my creative intellect feels restless. It's not just about being busy, it's about being busy with challenges you *want* and are stimulated by. Activity doesn't always equal intellectual challenge. And if you are creative – you can get more creative with your fears and fear responses, if you don't give your mind other tasks and focal points.

Structure

We all need structure in our life and to focus our time on the things we value. If you have a diary that has room for fucking around you will give growing space to anxiety. Goals that are compelling and a busy week full of things to think about will keep anxiety at bay. Putting extraneous data in our brains reaffirms its presence. It sounds mad, but for some people, the first step to a cure is to stop dwelling on it. Spend time letting your brain try something new instead. If you don't satisfy that intellectual hunger by closing the gap in which it grows, the anxiety will spread like mould. We need to reprogramme our genetic pre-disposition with non-anxious thoughts, forcing the anxiety control centre and the amygdala to believe that we are safe. Since boredom is anxiety's biggest ally, we need to be intellectually busy as well as being physically busy. Whether it is reading, planning a trip, learning to play a new instrument, starting a new business, beginning a new relationship, taking classes in martial arts or writing a book, we need to fill that void with purpose and stimulation.

Diversion and distraction are two different things. Diversion is when there is no room in your life for false risk assessments because you are too busy living it. Distraction is something we consciously do, like me creating a course in my mind while I was in a claustrophobic MRI scanner. Consider both diversion and distraction vital parts of your toolkit.

Exercise

F.E.A.R is an acronym for False Expectations Appearing Real.

Make a list of five things you have catastrophised that never happened.

Rethink – When Things Don't Go to Plan

Mind vitamin

Just before I was about to go on holiday to Dubai, I ripped my pectoral muscles while doing jujitsu. After the injury I thought about what I could no longer do, like not being able to skydive over the Palm Hotel as I'd planned, or go to the waterpark with my daughter. Unless I wanted to torment myself, I knew I had to change the way I thought about the injury, so I started writing down the positives, the upsides as well as the negatives.

Once I'd stopped whingeing, having allowed myself to express the negatives and get them out of my system, I considered the things I could do to speed up the recovery, and then I looked for any possible benefits of taking some time out from the sport:

- *Because I couldn't drive with the injury, I would walk everywhere with a weighted vest on. My mind and body was going to benefit from a new type of exercise.*
- *My wife wanted to get shredded again, so maybe she could walk with me, and it would give us more time together.*
- *Time out would allow other little injuries of mine to fully heal.*

It helps if you can starve the negatives as much as possible in order to let the positives through, focusing on the upsides of what you can do rather than what you can't. For instance, when I stopped drinking for the first time I stopped following all the feeds of my mates posting drinking sessions on social media for a while. In that way I wasn't always focusing on what I was missing. It's not easy, it just takes practice.

Life is full of unpredictability and things can go south for us at any time. Every day is a game of Russian Roulette between good and bad luck. However, the way that we respond to things going wrong is one of the few things in life that we have agency over; in other words the only thing we can control is how we respond to it. If you live in a hurricane corridor you have the choice as to whether you prepare your cellar for the next twister coming your way or doing fuck all. Putting your head in the sand is not going to help anyone much.

Planning for the worst

In this chapter, I'm going to talk about the Stoics again, because their advice on preparing yourselves for when the shit hits the fan is unrivalled in its pragmatism. While I am a great believer in visualisation and operating on a positive high frequency, we can't just sit there hoping everything will work out without lifting a finger. By now we should all know that life throws things at us randomly, but there are things that we can do to prepare for the worst.

Premeditatio malorum is Latin for 'prepare for all evils'. Stoic thought asks you to visualise in a negative way the things that could go badly wrong in your life. You don't want to spend too long doing this because thinking of dark foreboding situations will make you feel like a bucket of shit, but in feeling like shit for a brief, controlled time you experience a taste of the price you're going to pay if you do nothing to prepare. And this should help propel you into action.

For example, your parents are getting very old and don't have money put away for a funeral. So who is going to pay for it? Ask yourself how you will feel as their son or daughter if you have not put money by to ensure they have a nice coffin or that you can pay for the kind of service they want – whether that's a party and a free bar or a simple woodland burial as the sun sets. Just by thinking of this and sitting with the unpleasant feeling and moving past it, it will give you the urge to get prepared, get real and start putting money aside for when the time comes, as it surely will. At least you will be able to honour your grief for their passing rather than ignoring it until the terrible time comes when you lose a parent and have no choice about how to say farewell.

I was talking to a friend of mine the other day who was moaning that not enough customers were coming through their door at work because of high interest rates; he sells garden materials and sheds, and recalled the product flying off the shelves during the low-interest era, which seemed to go on for years until recently. Now, sadly, people are worried about the expense of beautifying their gardens and so are tightening their belts. My friend now regrets not shoring up enough cash reserves for when that interest rate dip would finally be over. If he had employed *premeditatio malorum,* preparing for evils – or rather, a change in the economy, which is never fixed and forever goes from low to high and back down again – he would have anticipated this outcome and taken action.

If you do prepare for the worst that can happen, when it arrives at least you will have some kind of plan as to how you are going to react. The Stoic Seneca said: 'What is quite unlooked for is more crushing in its effect, and unexpectedness adds to the weight of a disaster. This is a reason for ensuring that nothing ever takes us by surprise.

We should project our thoughts ahead of us at every turn and have in mind every possible eventuality instead of only the usual course of events.'

Chris Hadfield is an American astronaut who wrote a book called *An Astronaut's Guide to Life on Earth*, which is about his preparation to go into space and then his actual time at the International Space Centre. For years, he and other astronauts were prepped by NASA for specific technical things that could go wrong and forensically applied themselves to fixing each possible mishap. A little bit like 'forewarned is forearmed', rehearsing for many curveballs enabled Hadfield to be more relaxed and productive in his work, safe in the knowledge that he had the necessary experience to be able to deal with anything related to the space centre. I don't think many of us would ever imagine we'd reach Seneca's levels of nothing ever surprising us – but we can aim for Chris Hadfield levels. If you've prepared for all the problems you think you might have, you'll have more time, headspace and expertise when you inevitably have to tackle the problems you've not anticipated. Even if you've planned everything down to the last detail, accept that you cannot control life and there will always be something that will be thrown into the mix that wrongfoots you. But knowing you've thought through other challenges gives you confidence in tackling the unknown.

Things going wrong is part of life's journey. Another Stoic saying is 'The obstacle is the way'– meaning, there is great merit in welcoming and defeating a difficulty that stands between you and success. And you should view it like a gift and a challenge to be met and welcomed, because you can learn so much more about yourself, your resourcefulness and inner strength in how you dealt with it, rather than if it's all just plain sailing. You tend to appreciate things which are hard-fought for more than those that arrive as simply as an Amazon package at your door. If we can flip our thinking on curveballs and start to see them as an invitation to growth rather than life targeting us, we experience less fear, less panic.

And when we've got through the crisis? There's room for analysis as well. 'What went wrong?' doesn't have to be a negative question, but an enlightening one. Shine your torch into the dark corners – don't just slam the door and hide.

Don't rely on willpower

When I ask clients 'What went wrong?' nine times out of ten the answer will be an external influence – an unexpected situation, a person or circumstance that has become a roadblock. But outside acts of God or shocking tragedies, the real issue is often our own motivation. Did you not complete your running training because your laces broke or it was raining – or because you couldn't talk yourself into getting up when your alarm rang?

Willpower is unreliable as fuck and has an expiry date. It'll be fine for a while, at the start of a challenge or when you wake in the morning with a new resolution, but by the afternoon it will have gone. You've seen already that Upgrading is not just easier but almost inevitable if you make your circumstances deliver it rather than your willpower. It's much more reliable to set up your environment so you can win, controlling the things that you see and paying attention to the people that you're with, even if it's only for a short while.

When I was in Dubai I removed myself from the skydiving hotel so I couldn't see other people doing it and start feeling sorry for myself. While on that holiday I saw quite a few professional football players, one of whom was on crutches. Andres Pereira had just had surgery. I looked at him with a big smile on his face (I'm sure he wasn't thinking about how much he was still being paid per week despite being injured) but he seemed happy to be there even on crutches and that pepped me up, made me think, other people are injured too, it's up to me to change the way I think and then feel about my environment.

While I was away, I needed something to focus my attention on, so I set myself a goal of 150,000 steps per week with a minimum of 20,000 per day. When you walk it makes you feel so much better. Not only are you working off calories as you do it, it also clears the mind – it's hard for your thoughts to stagnate if your feet are moving, your view changing. It also makes you check your privilege. Sure, I had a torn pec, but I could still get up and going. If you're lucky enough to have sufficient health to go for a walk, then take that opportunity whenever you can – even for a short walk. It's one of the lowest barriers to entry forms of physical exercise and wellbeing there is – tell yourself you'll just go for two minutes and I bet you go for ten.

Obviously, the torn pec wasn't my first rodeo when it came to something going wrong in my life. I learnt way back that when you're experiencing emotions you don't like it's purely because of what you're focused on. We're complex creatures, usually feeling more than one thing at one time. Don't like the way you're feeling? I bet another part of your brain is feeling something else. Give yourself the credit that you can multitask feelings.

Emotional transformation

When something doesn't go to plan, you think negatively about that thing and then experience a negative emotion, or sometimes vice versa – feeling then thought. I began to reframe these negatives as alarm clocks, emotional feedback rather than emotional punishment. Even this act, putting a moment between how you feel and how you react is powerful. Then I ask what are the facts behind this negative emotion? Are there any? Is there any evidence to back this feeling up? I can't change the facts, but I can change how I feel about them. I ask myself, what have I learnt? What are the benefits of this alarm call, what is it flagging up? I try to write down at least ten positives or advantages. Ten hidden gems. Ten obvious benefits. I do this so often that I find it easy. And by the time I've made my list, the initial stab of sharp feeling has usually passed and I've got some clarity back. And don't think I'm trying to be all happy-clappy. I won't pretend a shitshow is all fine and dandy. What I'm aiming to be is neutral. It's not about feeling positive, it's about getting neutral and clear-sighted.

Stripping away the intensity of the negative feelings

The power of NEUTRAL is another Upgrade key. If I only focus on either negatives or positives, I'm likely to overbalance. It's easy to get stuck zig-zagging across your path, when actually if you can keep yourself neutral, you can power forward. Neutrality is often given bad press but it can really be the sweet spot. It's not about self-delusion or sugar-coating the pill, nor about beating yourself up and weighing yourself down with regrets. It's about being able to look at the situation that's bothering you more objectively. It's freedom from drama. People think that when they're not positive there's something wrong with it. This is a problem, people thinking that everything should be one-sided – it's just not realistic. The idea that you must be broken if you're not completely happy isn't helping anyone.

Humans are machines with lots of clever mechanisms to get us back to balance – sleep resets our energy, homeostasis balances our bodies, but we often don't give our minds the same chance to get back to equilibrium. Don't fear the things that push you off track – life is about being pulled off balance, understanding this and correcting yourself to get back on course, not panicking that you're broken by every setback and spiralling into despair. By learning to become neutral and less dramatic in our thoughts, we start to focus on what we want to feel rather than magnify what we don't want to.

Somebody asked me this week, 'Why is my first thought of the day when I wake up always negative?' You might have heard people talk about the universal law of polarity, the notion that there is an opposite for everything, which is necessary for balance within our universe. Everything has a duality, and a built-in opposite cannot exist without the other; good and bad, life and death, love and hate, night and day, pain and pleasure, strong and weak … negative and positive feelings are both part of the same yardstick, one cannot exist without the other. So, the more that we try and recognise negative emotions as one side of a coin, the better we can make an informed decision on how to flip that coin over and ensure that negative outcome doesn't happen.

I used to think that my wife was what many people might term pessimistic, but actually what she was – and still is – is really good at spotting possible things that could go wrong that I might have missed. She doesn't trust anyone, whereas I trust everyone, which means we've got this balance that we achieve with each other's opposites. Because she's more risk-averse than me, that stops me making rash decisions. Just as in my office, we have people that are loud like me and others that are quieter. That's just as well, because if you had a team who were all like me it would be explosive!

Don't get me wrong, I'm not for a moment suggesting that we should carefully divide our employees into an exact 50-50 between extroverts and introverts. Far from it. In fact, I don't believe we're either extrovert or introvert, I think it depends on the situation we are in at any given moment. A judge used to delivering life-altering sentences might freeze if you asked them to tell a joke in public, or the loud-mouth at the back of the bus might fall silent if they had to speak at a funeral. The loudest most confident person in the room is often much more insecure than they seem and are simply pretending to be something that they're not. So, an extrovert may not be a natural extrovert, but one that has developed a projection of themselves as such.

My co-writer, Rich, used to be far more extroverted than he is now. It's interesting that his period of extroversion coincided with him being an actor. He acted in a more extrovert style because he thought that was the most obvious style for an actor in order to stand out. These days, as a writer, he is much more introverted but comfortable with that style, because he's not positioning himself as something he's not.

Back in 2021, I'd been diagnosed with Long Covid. I was running an event and I just wasn't feeling it. I remember saying to my wife Leslie that I felt exhausted and just didn't feel like being the showman that night. Her response was really interesting: 'Paul, you don't have to be the showman every night, allow someone else to rise up. You're used to being the person in the room that everyone looks to and draws energy from, why don't you sit back.' Don't get me wrong I love what I do, but sometimes you feel under pressure to be the one that raises everyone else up.

Sometimes, when I'm not massively energised and perhaps have a cold or some other physical issue that is slowing me down a bit, I now share it with my audience and they love it, because it makes me more human. People ask me often on Instagram if I am always this positive? And the answer is no. Nobody can be positive all of the time. But the reality is I love what I do, and I will show up for it however I am feeling.

Loving what you do

Loving what you do means you embrace the positives and the negatives, the pain and the pleasure, the upsides and downsides, the criticism and the praise, the support and the challenge, because you're on your mission. Why should we love the downsides? Because we have to; you can't love anything that you don't know both sides of. It's like that old chestnut: *every cloud has a silver lining*. In other words, every downside has an upside. When you're on board with your purpose and heading in the right direction, negatives don't worry you. After all, no river ever ran in a straight line, did it?

I drew inspiration from Conor McGregor in his Netflix series *McGregor Forever.*

When Conor pulled a ligament in his knee, he had to take twelve weeks off training and sparring. He had to go into battle with depression daily. 'Without something to work towards, a goal, it's tough.' But he made sure he kept in shape doing other things instead. He said, 'Nothing good ever comes from sitting on your own feeling sorry for yourself and worrying about things.'

When you're known as a fighter like Conor, you have to believe you will win, but also know that losing is part of every fighter's journey. He says, 'In order to succeed as a martial artist you need to lose loads of times. Win or lose I will take something from it all.'

We hold up our fighters as supreme physical specimens – but it's their mental strength that really marks out the champions. When asked what the key to success was, Conor answered: 'Ninety-five per cent mental, five per cent physical.'

When the media follows fighters, it's often the trash-talking that gets coverage. But as Conor McGregor's series shows, as well as Arnold Schwarzenegger's *Arnie*, both of these powerhouses are seriously good at self-talk. Schwarzenegger talks about how as a young man he dreamed of being a champion bodybuilder and how he imagined everything that would happen to him in the future, how it would happen, how he would meet his bodybuilding hero. Both Conor and Arnie have fertile imaginations to practise visualisation and a strength of vision that meant even when things didn't go to plan, they weren't put off.

Even when he was just starting out as a fighter and still claiming benefits, Conor McGregor was already planning his path to victory and UFC domination, while Schwarzenegger was still living in his little Bavarian town dreaming of becoming Mr Universe. But still, both of them pictured every detail of their triumphant future.

Exercise

List three things that you currently dread happening and explore how you can make the best of the situation should it happen.

Nailed it – Fixing Your Goal to a Process

Mind vitamin

The concept of SMART (Specific, Measurable, Achievable, Realistic, Time-based) goals that you've probably come across on work training courses or self-help videos is flawed. The bit I don't like about this is the idea of a realistic goal; when many of us don't hit our goals, it's often not because they're too hard, but because they're too accessible and don't excite us. Our biggest successes in life come when we overcome huge odds, things that at some point we thought we couldn't do but we did. And at one point that target was an unrealistic goal.

Instead, I think we've all got a licence to dream big. An unrealistic goal is one that scares you a bit, is beyond your current level of ability, inspires you, lights your inner flame, impacts other people, forces you to grow. But here's the crucial part. I'll share how we tie up and make this seemingly unrealistic goal manageable. We create a realistic process, time frame, system and plan based on where you're currently at. It's process that is the way we Upgrade ourselves.

Here are a few questions we can ask that will help nail our goal to a process quickly and effectively:

- *Who has already done this, who can open doors for me?*
- *Why is this important to me?*

- *Who can help me?*
- *What are the steps to achieve this goal?*
- *What's the cost?*
- *What do I need to start doing, what do I need to stop doing and what do I need to keep doing?*

The challenge with an unrealistic goal is that you might think, 'It's too hard' or 'It's too far away' or 'It will take too long.' A process is what brings it all within your reach.

One thing that I see many people struggling with is the concept of goal-setting. Not just the shiny idea of it, but the nuts and bolts. Now I'm sure if you're reading this book then you've probably got the importance of goal-setting by now – having something to move towards. It's not just about the goals, or the targets and the outcomes of the mission. It's the energy they give you. But there can be a flip-side. I believe that people are unhappy because their reality, their life, doesn't match the mental pictures of how they thought it would turn out. And this disconnect between imagined and actual presents a problem. The problem is that they have no real clarity around how they would like it to be, so they focus on what they don't like about their life and the results they don't want, and that just becomes a never-ending circle of general unhappiness, lethargy and apathy.

Choose goals that really stretch you

The challenge with goal-setting, and the achievement of those goals is that you have to set the bar at the right height; not so high you'll never crack it, but not so low that it's a walk in the park. If you're not a little intimidated and unsure about whether you can complete it, it's not the right goal. I've already showed how working out how you want to feel is as important as what gives you that feeling, so work out what gets you most excited – the 'what' of your goal or the 'why'. Once you've got the first in place, the second should follow. Then you can crack the 'how'. Often you might have multiples in each category, but keep it simple and powerful and then it's easier to hold yourself to account.

Take my trek to Everest basecamp in 2024.

What: climbing to Everest Base Camp.

Why: to raise money for cancer treatment for my friend's daughter.

How: cost it, find someone to train me how to trek and climb in the UK, source an organised trek outfit in Nepal … then go!

It's too easy to become obsessed with complications around the *how*. So don't start at *how* – fix your *what* and *why* first.

Imagine that we want to lose weight, we immediately tell ourselves how we are going to do it, and then talk ourselves out of it before we have even started because it sounds too hard or uncomfortable: 'If I'm going to lose weight that means I'll have to stop eating my favourite foods and go to the gym and …' Suddenly you've lost your motivation. Whereas if you think:

What: I want to complete the Great North Run.

Why: To raise money for good causes and get back into running.

How: Get a step-by-step training routine and optimise my nutrition.

Suddenly you have clarity, motivation and purpose rather than threat and overwhelm.

The key to living an Upgraded life is defined by your vision of the future. I'm going to share with you how to create a really compelling three-year vision of where you want to be. Using a method that I call the 'red-hot hand technique' as sure as sharks like eating seals, you will soon feel inspired and excited about your future.

The red-hot hand technique

I am going to start a stopwatch and the timer will be on for fifteen minutes. The key to this working for you is that you do not stop writing. We're going to go well beyond what you'd normally write down for your goals, as chances are you have set the same ones multiple times, not even got started, or given up halfway. I'm going to take you beyond that with this tool, so you'll think well outside of the box and get a little bit more creative and inspired.

Stage 1

The chances are you've not written solidly for fifteen minutes since school – and even then you probably stopped to chew your pencil and stare at the clock. But not anymore. The timer will be on for fifteen minutes and for the duration of those fifteen minutes I want you to keep writing, imagining where you would like to be in three years' time as if it has already happened. To do this we are going to complete the following sentence: *'I am so happy and grateful for what I've achieved. My life has been a great success because . . .'*

It might be, 'My life has been a great success because . . . I've travelled to so-and-so, I have published a book, won a certain accolade, started a successful business, set up a charity, got to spend the weekends with my family, built a legacy, hang out with so-and-so, or get to spend four hours playing golf every day.'

If you stop, keep coming back to the same sentence: 'I am so happy and grateful for what I've achieved. My life has been a great success because . . .'

All the ideas you come up with will be useful, don't worry about what anyone else would put on their list or what they would think if they saw yours.

And if we get stuck here are a few prompts we can use:

- *Where* do I live?
- *Who* do I spend time with?
- *How* do I spend my time?
- *What* I do in my free time?
- *How* do I get paid?
- *Who* is in my peer group?

Okay, your fifteen minutes – and don't stop writing – start now. Go! Timeout, your fifteen minutes are up! How are you feeling? How did you get on?

That's not an easy exercise to do, but if you managed to keep writing you are probably feeling inspired, motivated and energised. Maybe you felt some nerves while doing it, maybe some butterflies of excitement? Imagine if you could create this uplifting feeling every day. Well, you can, it's just a question of creating a visual reminder; perhaps a screensaver on your laptop, or a screenshot on your phone of the goal you were particularly excited by. Having that in your vision is like knowing your destination on your satnav.

Stage 2

I want you to try and stay in this space of feeling inspired. Now that we've done the creative part and mapped out a destination we are going to become a little bit more mechanical. We're going to shrink this down from three years' time, to one year's time. And the question I'm going to ask next is 'How will I know when I am a third of the way there to achieving my three-year vision? What are the ten to twelve goals that indicate I am making progress?'

I'll give you a quick demo of this. I did my red-hot hand technique recently, and for Stage 2, I created these twelve-month bullet-pointed targets:

- My new book is written and contracted by a major publisher.
- 100 coaches pass through my coaching academy.
- Compete four times in jujitsu.
- Climb two mountains.
- Four phone-free holidays.
- A week-long retreat.
- Dubai skydive.
- Eat at four new Michelin-starred restaurants with my wife.

Now take five to ten minutes to bullet-point where you want to be in a years' time. Have a look back at that three-year vision and ask yourself the simple question, 'What would indicate that I'm a third of the way towards that three-year vision?'

Stage 3

We're going to shrink it down even more now. How will I know I am a quarter of the way toward my one-year outcomes. 'What would indicate that I'm a quarter of the way towards that year-off vision?' Write down five or six ninety-day goals. For example, depending on your business and lifestyle commitments, in the next three months you might:

- Buy a Porsche Taycan.
- Watch a match in London, Liverpool, Glasgow and Europe.
- Add one more property to-let to your portfolio.
- Start or complete a house renovation.
- Speak with at least three of my peers.
- Speak in three different countries, with my family there.

Stage 4

How will I know that I am a third of the way towards my ninety-day vision? What indicates that I'm a third of the way towards my ninety-day vision? Based on earlier distant goals, it might be taking a step towards them. For instance:

- Place order and deposit on a Porsche .
- Renovate the bathroom first.
- Identify and offer on one property to-let.
- Climb first mountain.

By making it small we make it so much more actionable and seem less far away in the future, without ever forgetting what we're ultimately working towards. For example, writing a whole book is intimidating because it's such a long journey and there is so much work involved, so imagine breaking it down into chapters, and tackling the first chapter. But before that chapter you have a paragraph, and before that paragraph you have a sentence, and this is how we start towards achieving our goal. Step-by-step but with an exciting end-goal always in our mind's eye.

Stage 5

What are the VERY NEXT steps?

Break it down into micro challenges:

- Look at tiles for the bathroom, find builder.
- Do a viewing on a property for sale.
- Start doing squats to build leg muscles up for climb.

Exercise

On a scale of one to ten, how clear are you on what's required to hit your goal and what's in the gap – what needs to change?

When the Clouds Roll in – Depression

Mind vitamin

Recently I was a keynote speaker at an event in Brighton with an audience of 1,500 people. I loved it. My energy was through the roof and I was buzzing with all the attention I was getting on stage, and the contacts I was making offstage. I must have taken 300 selfies. Given the excitement and the fact that I was on stage at eight in the evening, I was fizzing with adrenaline and so couldn't sleep much for the two nights I was there. I had to crash and burn at some stage, and I returned to the north-east in a low mood. I was just fucking exhausted. But the way that I dealt with this low mood was by recognising it and acknowledging it but keeping it at arm's length so that a part of me stayed neutral and recognised I was in a low mood without letting it define me.

I let the feelings be noted but after spending a little time in my pity party, the oh, woe is me, everything is shit *room, I knew I could let those emotions go and so I sat down and wrote a few questions and answers on a piece of paper.*

What emotion am I actually experiencing?

I'm feeling fatigue. The physical sensation of tiredness is affecting my perception of emotions.

What does that mean?

Well, I've been working flat out for the last couple of days, and I've emptied my tank. I jump more easily to negative interpretations of situations.

How do I want to feel?

I want to feel better: positive, energised.

What makes me feel better?

Massage, walk, swim.

Which one am I going to do and when am I going to do it?

I'm going to have a massage this afternoon.

Just by asking myself these questions I was able to isolate my state and spot why I was feeling like this, as well as finding a solution and committing to actioning it within a tight timeline. Fighting depression is about seeing the signs and understanding them, and then if you can, reversing them before they be come habitual. If you can practise this with low mood – and anybody can do it, it just takes a little self-awareness and action – then you can cut off some depressive spirals before they take hold. These days I can very quickly spot a mood spiralling from low to dangerously low.

I want to make it clear that I'm not writing this as a doctor – but as someone who's been a patient. If you're in crisis, do consult the experts. But if you're not sure what you'd call your mental state or have never really talked about it, knowing that there are so many of us with experience of depression can be a way of exploring the subject in a hopeful way.

There are many different kinds of depression. You might have clinical depression which presents as having a loss of interest in the world around you and a lack of pleasure in your daily activities, also an inability to imagine positive outcomes, and generally feeling worthless and restless. Short temper, withdrawing from your friends and family, and the inability to get out of bed in the morning, low energy and morbid thoughts are all common. Clinical depression can attach itself to somebody for most of their life, but can be treated with medication, therapy and exercise.

Bipolar disorder, or what used to be known as manic-depression, is a condition I have which gives you extreme mood fluctuations and sharply different levels of energy. One moment I'm manic, up and flying and anything is possible, my energy sky-high. In this mood I draw people to me like moths to a flame as I become super charismatic and euphoric. I'm very high, but for every high there is a dramatic come down; what goes up must come down. Then there's the depressed bit, where the lows can be dangerous, with thoughts of suicide and hopelessness. While there is no current cure for bipolar disorder, and science seems to suggest it's often hereditary, it can be treated with cognitive behavioural therapy (CBT), psychotherapy and drugs, such as lithium. Bipolar people are often very creative and prefer to weather the lows in order to experience the extreme highs. Notable people with bipolar include Stephen Fry and my pal Tyson Fury. There's plenty of evidence now that many famously creative people, as well as great scientists and innovators throughout history would today be diagnosed as bipolar, but it's only relatively recently that it's been both easier to identify and become acceptable to share.

There are also forms of depression which are shorter-lived and not chronic. You might experience an episode of depression that never repeats once you're out the other side. It can be circumstantial, psychological, chemical or a combination of all of those.

But what I warn myself and my clients about is the depression we can accidentally, habitually or wilfully create in ourselves. Even with my bipolar I don't like labelling it as 'my depression' like it's a badge I need to display, or a possession. Depression doesn't have to be a resident in your mental house. I believe that we are all energy in motion, and our thoughts are impermanent. I think happiness is a place that you choose to visit, but you don't live there all the time. The more you practise going there the easier it is to be a regular visitor and your visits become longer. But don't panic at the first sign of sadness or lack of motivation – you can experience a huge array of negative emotions and successfully tackle them without them settling into the fog of clinical depression. If you notice depression is becoming like a heavy coat you wear, a reason not to do things or to set new goals, then ask yourself if you're accessing all the help and tools you can before it really sets in. So many people with depression don't realise they're suffering from it and are missing out on support – but equally many people who aren't in a clinical state are quick to wrongly label a low mood as depression.

When I was clinically depressed, my wife had to drag me from the bed, and I'd be in tears, I just couldn't be bothered to do anything to help myself. I couldn't see the future as being a positive place where I imagined good things happening, it was just a blank, and the effort involved to try and identify the first thing that would make me happy was just too much. When you suffer depression it's like the colour is turned down so everything looks dull and monochrome, and noise is muffled and far away; in fact, everything is minimal and the opposite to being inspired. Depressed people cannot see a future. They feel shit and often can't or don't take care of themselves mentally or physically, which leads to more spiralling.

Some depressive conditions can't be avoided – especially hereditary or circumstantial. But some can be swerved altogether, and many depressive states can be helped or shortened. To do this, I believe there are three areas that you need to work on in your life to limit depression:

1. Environment. This is the external world around you and includes your 'inputs'– the things that you watch, the books that you read, the music you listen to, the people who you spend your time with, your support groups, the friends you surround yourself with, even the food you eat and the rest you give your body, because they are all the things that you are feeding into your body and mind. It's hard to get the output you planned when your input is not aligned with where you want to go.
2. Outputs. This refers to the actions that you're taking towards achieving your purpose and goals, including how you are taking care of yourself – exercising, meditation, conversations with positive people. You might need to drill down from your monthly plan to create weekly or daily plans so you can realise you are still moving forward – small, daily goals can get you back on course. A walk, a phone call, a piece of research – all of these are outputs that bring you nearer your vision, even when it feels far away.
3. Mindset. You'll notice I've put this after outputs not before! Sometimes you can be feeling terrible, but if you get on with doing something, producing some outputs, your mindset will catch up. You can't always wait for your head to be ready. But you can help it catch up – using positive language, visualising, reminding yourself of past successes.

When I gave the talk in the prison that I mentioned earlier, the point at which I noticed prisoners leaning forward and really listening was when I made the comment, 'You're trying to move forward and change your life, but you're constantly reminded of your past.'

When you have low energy, you are defined by your past. High energy most readily comes from visualising our future with passion and purpose.

If you ask a depressed person what they're working on, they will probably answer, 'Nothing' or 'Everything' – both can feel equally paralysing. If we stop pedalling, we fall over because of a lack of momentum. Seneca the Stoic, famously said, 'If a man knows not which port he sails to, no wind is favourable.' In other words, you need a frickin' plan. We have to create our lives and curate positive things, while cutting out the shit. That means being aware of negative influences, in many forms. Sometimes, it can even mean things that can be useful in other contexts, like the news. Personally, when I can feel depression trying to get its tentacles round me, I ditch the news in favour of interesting documentaries or specific articles that I want to read. It's a major way of managing my inputs. Watch out for how you respond to the news – especially when we're in an era of global turmoil. You can be well-informed without rolling news – consuming it once and consuming it well can be better than doomscrolling and snacking on headlines. You are allowed to switch off and sleep. Depression finds a way in and hits home when you are tired, your barriers are down and you're vulnerable not only to the headlines, but also to making and agreeing with negative thoughts generated by you. Actively switching off isn't putting your head in the sand – it's taking care of yourself to reset and return.

Exercise

1. When you feel a persistent low mood might be veering towards depression, what are three of your energy-creators you can engage in?
2. Note down three inputs that you feel nourish your body and mind in a way that works for you.

In Too Deep – Dealing with Overwhelm

Mind vitamin

Ask anyone what overwhelm is, and I bet they'll tell you it's too much of something, or too much of everything. I would like to put a fresh perspective on that. Why are people overwhelmed? Really the answer is 'lack'. They think they've not got enough of whatever they feel they need to tackle their inputs – focus, energy, rest, ideas, time. It's a feeling of not being or having enough to cope with what life is throwing at you. I'm sure there've been points in your life where you've experienced it, when you felt swamped by tasks, endless to-do lists with stuff building up constantly. Somebody who suffers from overwhelm is experiencing high negative energy, often hitting a point where they lock up or burn out. But remember, overwhelm is a state that we create, a stress response to volume or combinations of activities and demands.

Three things in particular contribute to it:

- *Physiology. When your energy is low, when you're out of shape, when you're just not in a healthy spot, it's easier to be knocked off your feet by the hustle and bustle of life.*
- *What are you focused on? Sometimes overwhelm comes not from the activities we're doing, the tasks we've set ourselves or been set,*

but when we zoom out and look at the bigger picture. That's a healthy habit – but if we keep zooming in and out too rapidly, we achieve nothing apart from overwhelm.

- *Language. There are multiple words for overwhelm – stress, challenge, overload – but don't let them mask the emotions underneath, which might point to situations that need specific actions to resolve.*

What if using the term 'I am so overwhelmed' makes the situation seem worse than it is?

What if you're not overwhelmed, but you're just not clear on your priorities?

What if your expectations aren't being met?

What if you're not actually overwhelmed, but you think it's a reason to stop?

What if you're not overwhelmed but you're just scared?

What if you're not overwhelmed but you just need to change your strategy?

What if it's not overwhelm and you just need to change the way that you see it?

Overwhelm is an emotion that we create. It's easy to lower our standards, talk ourselves out of continuing when we feel overwhelmed. We can go and watch Netflix or have a snack or drink instead. But it is when things get tough that the dramatic changes get made. Maybe overwhelm could be the emotion of growth? Maybe we can use it to help us let go of the unnecessary and choose what's mission-critical for us.

What if overwhelm is just a rumble zone, like the vibration area on a motorway which course corrects you when you're driving? To deal with it you must set your attention on your intention. What am I working on? Where do I want to go? Ask yourself are you taking care of your body to get you there? What kind of shit are you putting into it? Are you going to bed too late? Consider your morning rituals too. Can you use them to get your state up to eight out of ten? If you're not starting your day at an eight out of ten, then do what you need to do to get yourself up to an eight – hit a punch bag, take a cold shower, do a meditation, go for a walk, hydrate, do some journalling. Raise your state!

If you hit the ground running in an energised state, you'll be better equipped to tackle those feelings of overwhelm. Where does it come from? As well as the feelings of too much and too little that we've already explored, it can be tied up with fear; fear that we are not smart enough, that we don't have enough energy, that we don't have the knowledge … But these fears are always 'possibilities', 'maybes' and 'what ifs'. If we let them floor us without facts, evidence or good reason, it's poor mind management. Give yourself some credit that you can and will cope and it might give you the confidence you need to be able to sort and stack the demands into essential, urgent and optional or long-term. Overwhelm appears when we are not clear on our priorities and we think we have to do everything right *now!* And so instead we end up doing nothing but watching a cat ride an automated hoover on YouTube. When our to-do lists are endless, it's easy to find ourselves procrastinating and distracting ourselves with easier jobs on the list than the ones that will really change the game. Or, even worse, we don't think we can do it all so we do nowt. Nada.

If you've already reached the stage where you're running on adrenaline, coffee or doom, your mind might be too wired to think your way out of your current situation. Instead, take physical actions to support it too. Don't just create endless mental lists. Write down what your priorities are and how important they are on a scale of one to ten. Get it out on the page and out of your head.

I read a great book, *Essentialism: The Disciplined Pursuit of Less*, which explores how we take on too much and underestimate completion times. Greg McKeown, its author, says, 'There is a word for trying to do everything all the time. Madness! I truly feel like it's this perverse disease of thinking and it has an absolute monopoly right now. Do more. Two more. Get more. Fifteen more. More, more, more!'

Society has become obsessed with needing more, and it's driven by many things – our always-on media, messaging apps and emails – meaning we can be reached (and expected to respond) at all hours. Shopping websites that mean our whims can be delivered to our door within hours of scrolling; social-media sites like Instagram and Facebook on our smartphones. The only way to free ourselves from this is to develop the mindset of only doing things that are essential and doing them straight away.

First, we have to shift our mindset into a new way of thinking, one in which we always consider the trade-off before we accept a new opportunity. Accept too many opportunities and we end up overwhelmed – so be discerning, be very discerning. You are wired to socially cooperate, which means when asked to do a piece of work that you're not interested in, you will still often agree. When you pause and discern what the trade-off is to you personally – to your schedule and available time – you are in a better position to judge whether it is essential or not.

Greg McKeown suggests that we start using the term 'let me get back to you', rather than just agreeing on the spot. FOMO, the fear of missing out, makes us feel we have to grasp every opportunity, but that means embracing lots of non-essential things. So instead, try JOMO – the joy of missing out – on things which are only going to cost you more time.

Less can be more, so cultivate your time and how you fill it. Most of us underestimate the time it takes to get something done, so that entails doing less things and being more mindful about what we choose to do. Greg goes on to say: 'Life is not an all-you-can-eat buffet. It's amazingly great food. Essentialism is about finding the right food. More and more, it's valueless. Staying true to my purpose and being selective in what I take on results in a more meaningful, richer and sweeter quality of life.'

Break it down into digestible choices

Make things smaller! The thought of climbing a mountain, writing a speech or earning your first million can seem vast. But all of these can be broken down into first and next steps which are far less intimidating. If you've got two stone in weight to lose, think about shedding the first couple of pounds, not beyond. Unless you're planning on severing a limb, you're not going to lose that weight overnight, so just focus on what you need to do that day, that week. It's also worth matching the scale of tasks to the windows of opportunity you have to action them. Too often we spend more time dreading a task than it takes to complete it. What are we putting off that we could do instantly? Which tasks are bigger and need proper time blocking out to handle them?

Priority or preference?

The second reason we find it so easy to create this emotion of overwhelm is because of false timelines. It's not what needs to be done that's screws us, it's our expectations around *when* it needs to be done.

Our expectations are often so high when it comes to ourselves. And when we don't meet those expectations, we self-destruct and feel deflated.

So we have to keep asking ourselves – is it a deadline or a preference that I am roasting myself over? Of course, we all want our actions to be taken as quickly as possible but is it realistic? Of course you will want results as quickly as possible, me included. But is it a looming deadline, or a target imposed without due thought? Most likely it's a preference creating a false urgency that is stressing you out and making it into overwhelm. You need to take it at your pace. You also need to know exactly where you are and how things fit together in your plan, not in your head but in your schedule in front of your eyes which brings us on to strategic mindset.

Strategic mindset

Another common contributor to overwhelm is a lack of strategic mindset. We've talked about your actions needing to be rooted in what you must do that day and that week. Actions can only belong in the present. But your plans – they need to be connected to the future. Being able to look further down the path and know where you need to be in three months or three days' time is key. With my crazy busy schedule, strategy allows me to avoid overwhelm as I know exactly what I am doing and where I am going. Strategy is about making everything clear and broken down in front of you.

Having a strategy is about getting the chaos out of your head and onto the page before you. Unless you're a genius, don't expect to keep it in your head like some kind of spinning 3D model. For most of us it's far easier to see all this on paper. Every one of my working days is broken down into a structure and timeline. Trust me, there's nothing I hate more than all that minutiae, going through every day putting every meeting in, but I know that all this detail is preferable to not having any. I need this structure in order to be able to thrive on my free days. I love what I do so I make sure I'm only filling my week with essential meetings I am interested in or training gigs that inspire me. A disciplined structure allows me to have an amazing life – evenings free, working a four-day week and weekends off. To get here, I've had to learn to be better at expectation management, assessing how long the essential gigs and meetings will take. But by using radical honesty at that early stage I can commit to a schedule that not only can I keep to, but I can share with the people that rely on me.

Shift your state

If you continue to experience overwhelm, move; take a walk in the fresh air, take a cold shower, step away, whatever it is you have to do to change your current state. Be clear with yourself whether your overwhelm comes from doubting your capacity or your capability. If it's the former, get your calendar up and do what you need to do to make the planning work. If it's capability, and you feel you've bitten off more than you can chew, working out what you can do will identify where you need to bring in extra resources or skill, or check expectations around what you're delivering. You might think you need to deliver the *Mona Lisa*, when your client might be expecting just a rough first sketch. Whichever it is, analysing and then acting need to go hand in hand. Stop resisting. Resisting is two things rubbing together. In the case of overwhelm, we resist what we have to do, and then our thoughts about it.

Get into an 'abundant' mindset

Abundance means that there's more than *enough* and it's triggered by gratitude. If I can operate from a place of gratitude; being grateful that I've got clients emailing me, grateful of people giving me shit online, grateful I've got the ability to turn notifications off on this phone and check messages; if I can be grateful for all of that, then I can realise that having plenty to choose from or work with is better than not enough. What if you were grateful for these challenges? 'If I didn't have these challenges, I could have worse ones!'

You need an abundant mindset because a lot of these feelings of being overwhelmed are fuelled by a feeling of scarcity – the perception that there is not enough. Triggered by fear – scared that there's not enough time or opportunity, or they might not ask me again– and not enough energy, not enough people on my team, only I can do it, cook dinner, finish that job, etcetera.

Remember, there is always enough time to do what's necessary, what really deep down matters, what's really important to us. Once you realise there is time, you just need to pick what you will give it to, you can ask these two questions:

1. What would be possible if I allowed myself a little more time and could move this to tomorrow? It's not procrastination it's identifying a preference and finding abundance not scarcity.

I'll give you an example. I was supposed to do a training session on 'energy' on a Saturday. I'd been away on a trip and on the Friday I had been really busy with meetings. Then Friday evening I was at jujitsu. So Saturday morning rolls around and I've got to do some training on energy, which is the one thing I haven't got at that point. Guess how I started to feel? Yep overwhelm. I asked myself if this was a deadline or a preference? It slowed my mind down to a stop. I ended up focusing on what were the true deadlines and putting together shit-hot training that was ten times better than if I hadn't asked myself that question.

2. What else would be possible if I allowed someone else to take that on?

This is something so many people need to ask themselves more: what else would be possible if I allowed someone else to take that on? (For example, I delegate a lot of the stuff involved for my podcast: I don't edit it, I don't do the sound, I don't email you the link, I don't do any of the forms. I do the parts where I deliver my best value, and I trust colleagues to do the rest.)

Create an abundant mindset – you don't have to say no to your ideas if you can bring people on board to make them happen. So after your *what*, *why* and *how*, start thinking of the *who* – who can you delegate to do it. Then think of the pay-off of creating that leverage – more time to yourself, more time off, more money, more energy for you, more time to do other things.

In our shared society, we have got good at relying on people for their individual skills and expertise – lawyers, doctors, PTs – we trust people who have skills that we don't. But sometimes we reach a point where we need to let go of things we can do as well as those we can't. Just because we can do something, doesn't mean we should. Just because we trust our own skills, doesn't mean we can't trust someone else to do those things too, and free ourselves to deliver other aspects.

Trust

We've seen how overwhelm can come from fear and scarcity. It can make us catastrophise and ask ourselves terrible questions. The problem with overwhelm is that we often ask ourselves the question before we do the task, before we have any proof. 'Am I smart enough, strong enough, do I have time?' Sometimes, you just cannot know these things until you've done the task. So the quickest way to deal with overwhelm is to go through it. Action is the swiftest answer. The brain is a black and white questioning machine, and it will try and find the answer to the question you ask of it. As Tony Robbins says, 'The quality of your life depends on the quality of the questions you ask it.'

Exercise

1. Think about any scarcity beliefs that might be hanging around you and note them down. Did financial trauma happen to your family when you were a child? Has it stayed with you?
2. Are your fears around scarcity of resource – e.g. money, food, housing? Or about your capacity – e.g. your time, reputation, skills?
3. If you could do just one thing on your to-do list in the next ten minutes what would it be? How about the next hour, day or week?

People Pleaser – When to Say Yes and How to Say No

Mind vitamin

People need to know that you've got their back, and that they can turn to you for help and guidance. As my business started growing, more people were messaging me every day, so much so that I wasn't getting my own work done. It was 2018 and near the end of the year. Normally I'd run a ninety-day programme, but there was no time for a ninety-day programme, I didn't want to be working at Christmas, nobody did. Instead, I invented a course called the 'Six-week Sprint'. It was a resounding flop. Also, I was still getting all these direct messages and I started to feel overwhelmed because I couldn't read them all. If you want to stop chaos in its tracks, set up rules and boundaries for what you are trying to do. Every time I sat on my phone at night I was essentially saying no to playing with my children, or not spending time with my wife. On my Facebook page I stopped replying to everyone. There were still plenty of ways for people to reach me and for me to reach them. But this was one expectation I could reset. Rules and boundaries have changed my life for the better, you just have to adhere to them.

If you are going to live a life you love you've got to love people, and loving people begins with loving yourself. You will never rise beyond the opinion of yourself. Our biggest energy drains are people, or our thoughts of people. If I want to grow my business, I have to get better with people. If I want to make more money, I have to get better with people. People pay us money. If I want to impact people rather than be impacted by people, I have to be good with people. If you want to be a great parent you've got to get better at dealing with people, whether that's your spouse, your own child or their teacher.

I asked this question on my Facebook page – which kind of person would you like to learn to better deal with? The answers were as varied as the personality types that answered. But all the answers centred around the most toxic traits. How do we learn to deal with people that display those? The suggestions included the following: confrontational people, liars, cheats, victims, gossips, loud, opinionated, aggressive, unsupportive, obnoxious, narrow-minded, arrogant, nosy, needy and selfish people. Easy!

Often, we feel most at home dealing with people we perceive to be similar to ourselves. Which makes it tricky when it comes to negative traits. But it's not other people who are the problem, it's what we think of them that is the problem. We may want to control what people do, what they say, how they act. And when they disappoint us, we say we don't trust them. But you can't control other people (though you might be able to influence them) so when it comes to personal interactions, it's your responses that are yours to control.

Critical components

The three facets to remember when it comes to how we deal with people are:

Your state – how you handle people will always have something to do with where you are – physically and mentally. Let's face it, when it comes to tackling tricky people, we are all at greater risk of behaving like a bitch or a prick when we're tired. In this state we're more likely to get triggered by people. When your energy is high you are able to overlook and rise above idiotic people and focus more on your vision.

Your perception – you have to get used to thinking, *it's not them it's me.* It's not always about tolerating or having empathy for them (although that can go a long way) it's also about lessening your suffering so you can save your energy and put it onto something that you really give a fuck about. It's not about forgiving them. It's not what they've done that matters, it's what you make it mean; it's your perception. *It's not them, it's my thoughts of them.* It's also true that people who trigger us are those who mirror traits we have ourselves that we don't like. At times, we've all demonstrated negative behaviour, been aggressive, nosy, cheated, been unsupportive, obnoxious, victims, gossips, narrow-minded, or arrogant. When we see it in other people, it can make us look at ourselves uncomfortably. The people who push our buttons can be our greatest tutors.

Expectation – this is related to perception. We're all guilty of sometimes lazily assuming people should act like we do, have the same opinion as us, share the same worldview. But look at the reality first, their behaviour, what they actually did. Then consider what your expectations of them were. People can only let us down when we put them on a pedestal. When there's a gap between what we expect and what they are doing, there is the problem. When expectations and reality rub together they create friction.

Live and let live

Even when we enter a tricky social situation by checking our own states, our perceptions and expectations, it can still be hard to avoid conflict, anxiety or confusion. When I start to feel friction, I use phrases like: 'people are doing their best', 'stop picking a fight with reality', 'I can't expect me from other people'. Mantras are all about repetition, and if you say them enough you believe them. All of these mantras can defuse potentially confrontational situations by respecting people's shared humanity and not giving every interaction the heavy emotional baggage of expectation.

What is a people pleaser?

Of course, some of us can go too far when it comes to accepting everyone's differences. People pleasers put everyone else first, even at the expense of their own wants and wishes. They tend to draw their short-term energy from saying yes to people – but in the long-term it can cause resentment and burnout that deplete rather than produce energy.

You're a people pleaser if you:

- Find it hard saying no.
- Say yes when you actually mean no.
- Agree to something and then get resentful.
- Express how you feel and it is not reciprocated.
- Worry about annoying people.
- Don't ask for help.
- Feel guilty about doing the things you want to do.
- Expect people to know why you are unhappy.
- Don't like expressing your emotions or opinions.
- Have a difficult time standing up for yourself.
- Avoid confrontation.

How did you end up being a people pleaser? At some point in your life you probably sought out approval and praise and were denied it. My mum never gave me praise but only said what I wasn't good at. I remember one occasion that really hurt me. It was a parents' evening and afterwards she said, 'I'm never coming to one of these parents' evenings again, I'm so ashamed.' People pleasing comes from a fear of being rejected and from needing approval.

So we end up seeking out approval in other ways. We've learned that we get better outcomes when we serve and pacify other people's needs, because it gets us accepted, but then it becomes a habit. What makes it worse is the 'paparazzi effect' – when we think we're the star of everybody's show, that everybody is watching us. We end up contorting and constricting ourselves to try to meet what we think people expect of us: *what will they think of me if I don't do this, will they think I'm selfish, will they think I don't like them?* But actually, we're no one else's main character and I can almost guarantee they spend far less time thinking about you than you think. So stay true to your own course.

People pleasing is harmful for everybody because it makes you doubt or even lose your own path. If you say yes to something you really want to say no to, or because of fear of conflicts, it's harmful to everybody. If you're constantly agreeing to doing things you don't want to do, you may become overwhelmed or even passive-aggressive, which is a surefire way to poison relationships long-term. You will end up resentful and you may finally explode like a volcano.

If you carry on, you will compromise your health and happiness because of all the things you think you have to commit to. To top it off, you have to act like you are happy because you said yes to the things you now resent. All this springs from the fact you believe at some level that you are not good enough for people to like or accept your desires and priorities, so you downgrade yourself. If your definition of a relationship is that you always put the other person first, you need to find balance. If you feel guilty as fuck when you voice your wishes or needs, you need to start unpicking some habits. Because Upgrading means valuing your own needs as much as other people's.

Now, I'm not saying you can't be kind and thoughtful. We all like to be kind and supportive, we all go out of our way to help people sometimes. It's the 'sometimes' that's the key word here. It's great to put other people first on occasions – as long as it's not at the expense of your own physical or mental health, and as long as someone (whether that's you or others) is putting you first sometimes too. Also, make sure when you think you're putting someone first, you're actually giving someone what they want or need – not just your imagined version of it!

Watch out for the following common people pleasing beliefs:

Low self-worth. When we don't believe we deserve approval or importance. You feel your only chance of getting love and acceptance is to bend over backwards to serve other people's whims and needs.

Your beliefs around kindness and generosity. You can be kind and generous to a fault. You believe that your needs are always secondary, that self-care is negative, self-indulgent or unneccesary.

Confrontation is bad. You feel saying no is always bad. You would rather go with the flow and do something you disagree with because you don't want to rock the boat.

How to install new beliefs within us

If you don't believe people pleasing is damaging, then you're going to find it hard to stop doing it. You must instil the following belief into your mind: *to serve others we need to take care of ourselves first of all.* If I was low-energy, unmotivated and burnt out, and had zero time available to have my own adventures, the classic tugboat pulling everyone else but me forwards, you wouldn't be reading or listening to this. I live by setting an example. If my glass is only half full, how am I in a position to help you fill yours?

It's okay to love yourself, as when you do you don't need to people-please so much. How do we love ourselves? By paying attention to our positive traits, understanding that our perceived negative traits are valuable lessons in progress. By keeping our own inventory of our awesomeness, the stack of undeniable evidence that we are a good person, a stack of undeniable evidence that we are winning and are grateful. By accepting that our failures and missteps aren't eternal curses, just stepping stones.

This is about finding a balance. If you're only focused on your good points, that means you are infatuated with yourself, perhaps arrogant or deluded. If you only focus on your negative traits, that's being resentful of yourself. Balance and love is in the middle – yes, I have negative traits and I'm working on them, but I have positive ones too.

Communicating your own needs and opinion is a good, healthy thing to do. People pleasers, however, believe that communicating their opinion is aggressive. You have to realise that nothing bad is going to happen if you communicate what your needs and wishes are. If you still struggle, put yourself in your partner's position and imagine how hurt they would feel if they knew you felt unable to communicate with them.

How do I change my habit of people pleasing?

If you're a long-time people pleaser, it's likely something you've done so often you now do it unconsciously. And you're so used to doing it that others are conditioned to you either doing everything for them or always agreeing with them, so now they don't even notice or appreciate it anymore. It's become your and their normal. Decondition them by filling your life with things you want to do. Do be prepared for some pushback once you start protecting your time and energy. But first you've got to really notice where it's going. Writing is a great way to unlock this. When you start journalling you become more self-aware. You reflect on your actions and look at what's working and realise that it's vital to take care of yourself if you are going to impact positively on others. You realise that if you're not doing your morning rituals or taking care of your own needs and building your future, it's because you think the only way you can get love is to keep saying yes to things you don't truly want to do.

Stop one-sided relationships by not giving people space to keep taking from you. The important goals are the ones that impact other people positively. When I say yes to helping someone, I want to do it well and with the right attitude – not feeling resentful or rushed. If you're constantly saying yes to people, it means that you're often saying no to yourself. Do more for yourself and your goals and you will only have room to take on those things for others that you really feel are good causes, rather than duty-acceptances. Take a breath before agreeing to things – a moment to think about what you could be doing, what you know you should be doing, and what you are actually doing.

People pleasing is in the past

If you haven't planned a future you want to focus on that will impact well on others, you will keep saying yes in a scattergun way. When you're busy and focused on your future, it's easier to say no. Or, if you can't say no, remember you can just say nothing for a moment. Follow the five-second rule and remain silent to assert yourself and the automatic need to say yes.

Boundaries

If you're still struggling with saying no, it doesn't hurt to have some phrases up your sleeve:

- I'm not going to be able to help with this anymore.
- I'm going to have to stop doing that.
- I'm going to have to say no to that as I'm too busy.

It's not that you're saying you don't *want* to do something, it's that you *can't*. It sounds clear and firm from the outset. Like with so many of the topics we've explored, if you remember the 'why' then it becomes easier to action things that support that. When we are solid on why things matter to us, what we value, we know what needs to be protected.

The consequence of not being clear on what we value is people taking the piss. If we don't value ourselves and our own time, why would anyone else? It's okay for you to be strong and clear in your responses:

- No, I won't be available at that time.
- No, I can't move my other commitment.
- No, I'm not prepared to answer my phone at that time of the night.

Don't take it personally

You've probably been people pleasing so long you're totally focused on the people you're around rather than the actions you and they are delivering. Language is a powerful tool to course-correct that. 'I won't' sounds like you're refusing, but 'I don't' sounds like a policy, which is harder to push back against. The same way 'Sorry, I don't do that anymore', is clear, pure power – it even has a built-in acknowledgement which stops people arguing back saying, 'Well you used to . . .'

Adam Grant, author of *Give and Take*, has a very graceful way of softening saying 'no' which he calls 'relational accounts':

- If I help you, I'm going to be letting this person down.
- I'd love to help you move house, but I'd be letting my kids down who I said I'd go for dinner with.

This approach takes into account your plans with other people and that you don't want to let them down, and ensures you come across as a person of integrity. For people pleasers, it makes it easier to say no when we have a strong reason. It's also much easier for the person whose request we're turning down to receive. It establishes you as somebody who has boundaries.

Here's a parting quote to take with you: 'You don't have to set yourself on fire to keep others warm.'

Exercise

Make a list of three people you still resent because of something they said that you find it hard to let go of, then thank them for what the situation taught you.

In Your Head? Tackling the Fear of What Others Think

Mind vitamin

Not long after my audiobook was released, I was invited to a party thrown by one of the biggest publishing houses in the world. There were famous politicians, chefs, famous ex special soldiers, actors and of course loads of incredible authors. And I felt like I shouldn't be there, like I didn't belong. Like I was an impostor. There was champagne and a black-tie dress code and canapés galore – and it was all a bit too fucking posh for my liking. To tell you the truth, this big-mouthed northern bipolar idiot at this party full of famous people who talked very differently to me, texted his wife and said, 'I'm leaving, I have never felt so out of place before.'

The two people I knew who were coming had not yet arrived, and I felt like a spare prick at a wedding. Luckily, my wife gave me some Mort wisdom. Anytime we say 'should' or 'shouldn't' we are picking a fight with reality. I'd told her 'I shouldn't be here'. But I was there, I had been invited there, I hadn't climbed in over the wall – I'd published a book with the publishing house, one that was selling very nicely indeed – and so the 'should' and 'shouldn't' were irrelevant. I just had to stick to reality, not my feelings about it.

Just then, my publisher introduced me to a few people, then my agent and friend arrived, and I made some great contacts and I realised that there was no difference between me and these other people, I just hadn't been to a party like this before. And believe me, most of those people – even the great and the good – when faced by a wall of people they don't know feel that flicker of 'shall I just go?' – but jumping in is where you find the Upgrade.

This feeling of being caught out or not qualified, not deserving, is called Imposter Syndrome. I'm here to tell you, I don't believe it really exists because it's essentially just a label we apply to our discomfort. It's easy to label yourself with Impostor Syndrome, but curiously, real impostors don't believe they impostors, they are convinced that they are the real deal.

Somebody once sent me a message on Instagram that said, 'Paul, I've got impostor syndrome.' I wanted to ask, 'Who did you catch it from? What pills do you take for it? What cream do you rub on it?' It sounded like some kind of incurable disease. A self-prescribed label like impostor syndrome does not help or empower us, but it can become a crutch we can use as an excuse for not doing the work; staying comfortable because we're not ready to take the move into the discomfort which is where we will grow.

Impostor syndrome doesn't exist. It's an alarm to let you know that you're growing, that you're pushing yourself out of your comfort zone. It's a reminder that on the other side of this discomfort is something that you want. If you want to grow muscle, you have to get under the heavy bar. You have to feel the burn, you've got to lift it till you can't lift anymore. What do you get on the other side of that? Stronger. Fitter. More assured. Upgraded.

I try not to fight with who I am. The more that your behaviour reflects your authentic, inner self, the happier you will be in life. It's when we try to be something that we're not that we send mixed messages to those around us. Being at peace with myself is about owning my weaknesses and celebrating my strengths. It's about accepting my insecurities, instead of trying to hide them. So, for instance, I'll make jokes about my accent, I'll make jokes about how fast I talk, and also about the need to be the centre of attention, which is also an insecurity, but I own it by talking about it. I embrace my little bits of insanity. I don't try and fit in with everybody and I'm fine with people not liking me or the way I dress. I don't need or expect everyone to like me. I just need to reach the people I know I can help.

That's not to say I try to be purposefully provocative. I don't try to shock people with my swearing, because I don't swear on purpose, but if I do swear and it comes out of my mouth, then so be it. This is not me thinking *I'm perfect*, far from it, this is just about me accepting who I am, and so long as it's not negatively affecting somebody else, allowing myself to be me. I don't use 'I'm just being me' as an excuse to be a dick. Considering other people's feelings is normal and healthy and displays a level of conscience, of shared human endeavour. When you're aware your behaviour and actions are having negative impacts on others, but you have no care or thought for their feelings, that puts you in psychopath, sociopath and narcissist territory. So, you can be true to yourself without being a jerk – it just means making sure the real you isn't a total asshole.

It's hard enough being comfortable in your own skin without trying to project something you're not. You can *aspire* to be more patient, more tolerant of other's views and practise sticking up for yourself, being more attentive, etc. These are all traits we can improve, but you don't have to wait until you've mastered them all before you make peace with yourself. Pretending to be something you're not – hiding your thoughts or feelings because you worry what people will say or think – just isolates you and makes you feel half of who you really are.

Or perhaps you feel unsure who you are – it takes practice to hear your inner voice, feel your instincts and intuition.

I knew a guy who went to a boarding school because his parents lived and worked abroad. He was shy, quiet and had been bullied, and although he changed school for a fresh start, the scars of the trauma were already deeply embedded in his psyche. In order to never repeat that horrible time of isolation in his life, he went out of his way to fit in with a crowd, people pleasing and going with the flow. So much so that he ended up diminishing his self-respect and suppressing his real self to better fit the identity of the group, eventually following them down a route of too many pills and lines of coke long enough to fill the gaps between the white stripes on the M6 motorway. He lost his identity and thought he could only be himself when he was drunk or under the influence of drugs. Sometimes we have years of damaging behaviours to strip back to connect to our authentic self.

That isn't to say that our 'real' selves are something set in stone. We should change and grow as people. Our story can change with us. Sometimes when we have grown, we're acutely fearful of being rejected precisely because we're not the same predictable creature we used to be.

Neuroscience has discovered that the feeling of hurt we experience in social rejection shares the same neural circuitry as that with which we feel physical pain. Painkillers like morphine, when used in small doses, can reduce social pain, just as anti-depressants have been known to alleviate physical pain. When we pretend to be something that we're not, it stresses us out mentally and physically in the same way that lying does. People who have affairs and balance two lives, often end up in counselling with high anxiety because they are completely exhausted from spinning plates and spinning lies. Eventually, the plates smash, the web of lies gets too tangled.

What does leading an authentic life mean?

When our needs are met and we feel a sense of fulfilment and connection with ourselves and others and the world around us, we are living an authentic existence. The Roman Emperor and Stoic, Marcus Aurelius observed that, 'We all love ourselves more than other people, but care more about their opinion than our own.' The Stoics also acknowledged that the only thing that we can control is our approach to a situation, or our response to it; we have no power whatsoever to control or influence the response of another person or how they act. Rather than obsessing and magnifying out of proportion what other people think of us, we should recognise that most people have got their own shit going on in their heads and don't have the time to make critical judgements about us.

When we begin to turn our attention back on our inner selves and get to know our interior world, our weaknesses and strengths and the triggers that make us feel anxious, we also identify what makes us feel happy – what we are in flow with – and we begin to rely less on others and realise that everything that we need in order to live life as our true self lies within us.

When you start to consciously embed this thought in your mind you realise that you don't need to please everybody, that by just being yourself you can be much more happy, and self-reliant and successful as a free individual.

If I asked you to think about someone who pisses you off, before you know it, your talking becomes faster, your temperature has gone up, and you're feeling genuinely pissed off. Conversely, if I asked you to talk about something you've done this week that you are proud of you start to feel and be more confident as you talk about it.

Exercise

Think back to a social situation you dreaded that turned out better than you feared?

What did you worry would happen? And what gave you the confidence to get through it?

Look back at this when you've got an event coming up that worries you. Remember – you've survived 100 per cent of the parties, speeches, dinners or social events you've dreaded!

Tune in – Find the Right Frequency

Mind vitamin

Nikola Tesla, the Serbian-American physicist, engineer and inventor, famous for his work on electricity and energy (and who Elon Musk's electric car company is named after), once said, 'If you want to find the secrets of the universe, think in terms of energy, frequency and vibration.'

Great energy is infectious. When I'm in the company of somebody who is excited about their own future, they give off a good vibe and I can't help but be drawn into their positive energy. We hear the word 'frequency' and we probably think about tuning in the radio. But these days the science of sound and the frequencies at which we operate on are the subject of great scientific investigation. Just a quick visit to YouTube reveals a wealth of different pitches of sound you can listen to that have different effects on the brain – uplifting, inspiring, focus-improving, sleep-inducing tones.

When people are operating at the right frequency, others are drawn towards them like iron filings are to magnets. We've always had words for it – charisma, charm, good vibes – whatever you call it, you know it when you're near it. I really feel that when you show up with the right attitude, with real presence of mind, your magnetism grows like a benign force field – a halo of energy extending around your body.

There's hard science here too. Meditation involves slowing down your breathing, which allows your brain waves to slow down too, so that your mind is in concert with your body. When you're stressed your breathing is shallow and rapid and there's a lack of coherence between your thinking and what you're feeling. This is when your fight-or-flight mechanism kicks in, because it seems to your brain that your higher mind doesn't know what to do so it takes over with its basic programme-response system. The quickest way to get out of Cortisol Avenue, that place where you're feeding your stress with fear and anxiety, is by slowing everything down, and that starts with your breathing. As soon as we break the circuit of stress, like focusing on our breath, we're able to place the brain in a neutral, calm position where it's ready to analyse, notice and create. When the rhythm of your heart falls into step with your mind this is coherence; *a state of flow.*

At our most fundamental, we are all just energy. And I am convinced that we attract back to us the same energy we function at – we bounce back whatever emotions we are putting out to the world around us.

'Manifesting' is the new buzzword and its omnipresence might bore the crap out of you because everybody is talking about it. But fucking hell, Mush, it works! Most of you will have heard of Rhonda Byrne's book, *The Secret*. Its central tenet is that if you consider your life as one that is not blessed with luck and abundance, but as a place of lack, where you are just in survival mode trying to get by – firefighting, struggling – that is all you will attract back to you. Angst. And of course, the same is true in reverse – you need to be positive to attract positivity.

Visualisation

If all that sounds a bit overly mystical to you, what we are simply talking about here is visualisation, which in its purest form involves *feeling* what we are picturing in our mind.

Sportsmen have been doing it for years, imagining themselves not only winning, but at each stage of the competition mentally planning how they will *feel* and what they will do.

When we imagine clearly in our mind something we want, it produces a corresponding feeling in the body. This feeling in turn creates a physiological shift in our state, and our brain, unable to tell the difference between a feeling which is produced by something we have imagined and a feeling directly produced by something that is actually happening, then goes into overdrive to make it happen.

Strange but true, when you imagine something and how it makes you feel, your brain has no idea whether that mental construct is real or imagined. For example, imagine a swimming race that you are preparing for and break it down into stages; getting a good start off the blocks, having plenty of energy, executing a really slick tumble turn and pushing off against the wall giving you a clear lead, and then winning by a clear margin. You imagine how you're feeling in your moment of triumph; victorious, generous to your fellow competitors, grateful, happy … All these things need to be experienced in detail as if you are colouring in a drawing of the scene; you'll need to picture the crowd, that life affirming feeling of having smashed it. Revel in it, enjoy it. See yourself on the podium receiving the gold. It's that level of detail you want.

Going back to our friend Dr Joe Dispenza, whose work centres around this idea that our thoughts and beliefs create the reality we live in day to day. Dispenza says that the only way to change that reality is to actively examine these thoughts and beliefs, rejecting those that are no longer relevant or that are self-sabotaging, and replacing them with a clear set of new beliefs focused around who we want to be and how we want to feel. Getting rid of old habits that reinforce our unconscious states takes regular meditation and precise visualisation. Dispenza calls this, *mental rehearsal*, whereby we install the neurocircuitry in our brain so it matches our behaviours to our intentions. He says, 'The latest research supports the notion that we have a natural ability to change the brain and body by thought alone, so that it looks biologically like some future event has already happened. Because you can make thought more real than anything else, you can change who you are from brain cell to gene.'

It's a bit like creating a fresh route through a wood; at first, trampling through the undergrowth is hard work, but the more often we walk this path, the more established our footprints become and the clearer the route. Before we know it, this new path has replaced the old one by our repeatedly walking on it. Just as the more frequently that we repeat our visualisations, the quicker our desired and fully fleshed-out imagined reality will come to pass. Repetition of what we desire reinforces the circuits in our brain and forms deeper neural connections which then become habits.

The best way to go about getting really specific with your mental rehearsal is to ask yourself specific questions so the answers will then form your new set of beliefs and behaviours.

In her book, *Manifest: 7 Steps to Living Your Best Life,* Roxie Nafousi suggests what some of these questions should be:

- How do I feel in myself?
- What kind of relationships surround me?
- What kind of home do I live in?
- What is my profession?
- What am I most proud of?
- What do I want to change in my life?
- What do I want to keep the same?

Again, the clearer and more colourful the picture that we send to our brain with a corresponding feeling to match, the better. In order to really hone in on what we're asking the universe for, we should place our desires into organised boxes we can name: personal growth, career, domestic, health, hobbies and love. Consult your findings from doing the red-hot hand technique to guide you to your deepest desires.

Blisscipline

'Blisscipline' is my favourite recent discovery and has evolved from my study of Ishaya monks and their system of Ascension meditation, which helps you learn to rise above the self-limiting beliefs of yourself to discover the real you. Just like I turn to contemporary books and ancient philosophers to get the best insight from the best minds, I've immersed myself in a truckload of eastern wisdom and groundbreaking science, and from all this I've taken the best elements and put them in an industrial strength Nutribullet, and the result of this kick-ass spiritual and scientific infusion is my version of Blisscipline, the state where we are enjoying the work that takes us towards our goal, not suffering through it.

Reflecting on things we've done well is essential because it gives the brain compelling and unquestionable evidence and data, which then fills us with confidence and permission to keep achieving and reaching higher. It is essential that we believe in ourselves, and that we think we deserve what we are asking for. Confidence is the springboard to achieving your goals because it liberates the imagination to dream and visualise fluidly. Trusting in the power of your own mind is a way of discovering that your Upgrade is already within your grasp and not reliant on outside forces. If you're struggling to feel that power, I will always come back to meditation as a route back to it. I've had so many people dismiss meditation as 'too woo-woo' who have then been blown away by the results when I've convinced them to try it.

Six phase-guided meditation

Phase 1: physiological reset – in which we practise some deep breathing, contracting our muscles and then releasing them. Next, we set an intention of how we want to feel by the end of the meditation. Maybe it's that we want an idea by the end of the meditation or we want to feel relaxed or inspired.

Phase 2: getting present – we perform a guided body scan, imagining a warm flow as it works its way around our body. By distracting us from our thoughts for a moment, which are so often about the past or the future rather than the present, we can be in the now, the place where intuition lives.

Phase 3: active appreciation – when we picture episodes in our life where things have gone well, magic moments that we are proud of when we seemed to be in the flow, everything working in synch towards success. This is to get us to a place where we feel good, we feel inspired, feeling our power. Present, clear examples to ourselves of previous achievements, it suddenly makes the things we want to feel within reach, nothing is too big to tackle. We need to measure backwards and give ourselves illustrations of positive action: courage, determination, success, compassion, good sales numbers ... all these are the kind of evidence which breeds confidence within us.

Phase 4: pre-paving – some people call it visualisation, I call it pre-paving because it's like laying a clear path for your intention to follow – 'This is what I want, this is why I want it'. Having got yourselves in a confident place through Active Appreciation you're now in a position to envision abundance in your life and really believe in it. Scarcity is our default setting as humans, the inner voice that tells us, 'You don't deserve it, you are unworthy of such good fortune.' From that place, it's fucking hard to gift yourself a vision you really deserve, but when you come at it from a place of confidence you give yourself a licence to dream and imagine, and your self-doubt burns away to nothing in the brilliance of your vision. To manifest what you want, you have to imagine yourself doing, living and having whatever it is that you want; feel yourself really absorbing the moment, tasting it, noticing how good it makes you feel inside. These are the coordinates you need to feed your subconscious, which accounts for ninety-five per cent of our actions. But when given clear instructions by the conscious, your subconscious will believe and execute these.

Phase 5: allowing – this is when you sit with yourself and the feeling that you deserve everything you want to bring to your life. In this phase, people start receiving from themselves great ideas. I ask them to really try and pay attention and be open to synchronicities in the time that follows. For example, you talk about someone and then suddenly receive a call from them. I call these universal clues to remind you that you are on the right path.

Phase 6: laser focus – this final phase is about mentally priming ourselves for the day ahead, preparing for success. How do I need to think and feel today, what actions do I need to take? What behaviours do I need to demonstrate?

Exercise

To really supercharge your visualisations, write a list of prompts beforehand.

After you've been through a detailed visualisation come back to those prompts and write down all the extra details that sprang to mind as you went through the process.

People Like Us? Dealing With Different Personality Types

Mind vitamin

For the couple of years leading up to my attempt to take my own life in 2014, I separated myself from all the negative people in my life and moved to Spain. Except for my wife and son, I'd ghosted everyone. In time I came to realise that it's too easy to label people as energy vampires or negative; they are where they are and doing their best. When you imprint this phrase in your head it will completely flip the way you respond to them. When we look at life through a more compassionate lens it get easier. In Meditations, *his book on Stoicism, Marcus Aurelius writes, 'Say to yourself in the early morning: I shall meet today ungrateful, violent, treacherous, envious, uncharitable men. All of these things have come upon them through ignorance of real good and ill … I can neither be harmed by any of them, for no man will involve me in wrong, nor can I be angry with my kinsman or hate him; for we have come into the world to work together.'*

The ability to deal with any kind of person is a superpower. I built my business out from beginning with the people I knew best – guys like me who I knew would respond to the same tools that had changed my life. It worked well. But I knew there was more I could do. At the end of 2021, I started thinking that if I was going to grow my business exponentially, I needed to really open up to all types of people, because I was going to get all kinds of personality traits in the clients I was visualising. To improve my business and make it more profitable, I needed to remember that business is about more than numbers. It's built on relationships and connection with others. If two people are selling the same thing, who will the buyer choose? The person they like, trust, feel comfortable around.

If I want to improve my career, that means being able to find the best in people rather than the worst – to impact people and be impacted by inspiring people, yet also to not be too impacted by people whose priorities run counter to mine. If you want to have a better relationship with your partner, your partner's friends, your partner's family … you've got to make a true and authentic connection. This means you have to show up and engage where you can – no one should be on 'transmit' mode all the time, we need to be on 'receive' mode too. BUT it also means knowing when not to engage, when not to let other people's drama disrupt your path. If you've learnt the power of active listening (which is basically understanding rather than just hearing) you can rapidly tell the differences between when someone is looking for help with their situation or crisis – and when they just want fuel.

It takes all sorts

Hopefully by now you've quit people pleasing and have grown comfortable with showing up as yourself. It's this that holds the key when it comes to dealing with different personality types. Now, I'm not saying you're not different versions of yourself with different people – I'd expect you to chat differently to your nan than you would to your boss or your mates. But, the Upgrade key here is being comfortable with those different variations of yourself. You might have heard of code-switching – when people switch between different linguistic styles when they're in different company. It can go as far as speaking in different accents or dialects – and can be seen in the pressure minority groups often feel when outnumbered in a room, whether that's people who are made to feel conscious of their class, race or regionality in conversation. While it's fine that all of us probably have a 'phone voice' it's not all right to feel a pressure to be or sound like someone else. When you are confident of your purpose, you are thinking more about that when you enter a room, rather than what people expect you to sound or act like. And trust me, that confidence and clarity is key to interacting with different personality types. I've always respected the people who treat everyone with the same respect – if you're going in for a meeting with a CEO, you better be showing up and treating the security guard and the receptionist with the same energy and attitude you show the big cheese.

Bullies, instigators and ringleaders

As we've seen, most people aren't as difficult as we imagine them to be – they're just in their lane, doing their thing and it shouldn't throw you off course. But there are some people that because of voids or negativity in themselves, feed on drawing negative reactions from others. How do you face down someone determined to rile, mock or attack you? I go back to the old adage – don't worry about the opinions of anyone you wouldn't go to for advice. Put a space between their actions and your reactions. If they're looking for your engagement, you don't have to feed their fire – you've got enough spark of your own.

Flipping your thinking: Byron Katie

The happiest people in life seem to be those who don't overthink. Byron Katie, the author and speaker, was so depressed during her early thirties that she couldn't get out of bed for weeks, and then she had a sudden epiphany, a moment of clarity in which she realised that her suffering came directly from her thoughts about her situation. Thoughts like *my life is shit*, *I'm not a good person*, or *I don't deserve happiness* were about herself rather than the situation.

She realised that when she wasn't thinking she was happy, but when she did think, and indulged those thoughts, she became unhappy. This lightbulb moment gave rise to her designing a process of self-questioning known as 'The Work', and simply involves us asking ourselves four questions about each belief that is causing us pain. In the process, the idea is that we begin to realise that there is not just our version of the truth, but a number of others that might also be correct.

- Is it true?
- Can you absolutely know that it is true?
- How do you react when you believe that thought?
- Who would you be without the thought?

Following this, then flip with a *turnaround sentence* which is the opposite of what you believe. For example, a dominant thought might be, *I feel awkward around people because I don't think they like me.*

Now let's pose the four questions and answers to the statement, *I feel awkward around people because I don't think they like me*:

1. Is this true?

Yes, I think so.

2. Can you absolutely know that it is true?

Well, not definitely but they don't seem very interested in me. Also, I seem to clam up.

3. How do you react when you believe that people don't like you?

It makes me feel broken and isolated, like there's something wrong with me.

4. Who would you be without that thought?

I'd feel so much lighter and at ease in myself.

Now flip the original sentence, I feel awkward around people because I don't think they like me, with a turnaround sentence:

People feel awkward around me because they don't think I like them.

People don't feel awkward around me because they know that I like them.

I don't feel awkward around people because I know they don't like me.

Just by examining the alternatives, we can see that anyone of these may be true, not just the thought that we have come up with.

Every one of us has heard the expression 'It's all in your head' – usually said to us when we've latched onto an idea without clear evidence. The trouble is, we're all in our heads – we spend far more time with our thoughts than our external realities. Connection is what gets round this – speak to people, listen to people and don't just brood on what you think they're feeling. You can turn that mirror on yourself too – don't assume people know what you're thinking about them if you haven't said it or shown it.

Very often, it is our ego that gets hurt, bruised, by what we perceive to be slights from other people, which invariably isn't the case at all. It's just that the ego is a big diva who wants an Airstream trailer and a continual procession of people eager to kiss its feet. The ego is quickly offended and fails to see how it might be contributing to a situation or feeling.

Exercise

1. Write down ten examples of the ego taking over and causing trouble.
2. Is there a particular personality type you dread engaging with? Can you list why?

Procrastination – How to Make Taking Action Easy

Mind vitamin

Dr John Demartini says, 'We never procrastinate over things that are important to us.' I certainly never procrastinate over taking my son to football, booking holidays with my family, putting out useful content for people or doing one to one coaching.

At any one moment we live by a set of values, these dictate what we apply ourselves to and identify with. Whatever your highest value, that which matters to you most is how you identify yourself. It doesn't take much effort to do things we love. Things we require more discipline and motivation to focus on are of lower value to us and matter less to us, even if we pretend otherwise. And if you find yourself leaving big stuff you say you care about but pressing on with doing the small, meaningless stuff, it's probably because what you're really saying is that comfort is your highest priority right now and you're not prepared to get through the discomfort to get to the bigger rewards that come from bigger things.

If you confuse your high and low values, you will procrastinate over stuff and doubtless berate yourself for it. But if you prioritise your strength, passion and joy, that's where you'll find your authentic self. Don't live under someone else's value system because it won't resonate with you, you won't be able to get in flow with yourself.

Earlier this year I got injured when I tore my pectoral. I put on weight and got out of shape very quickly. I even grew a pair of man-boobs! I procrastinated over getting in shape, I procrastinated over my diet. Because I couldn't exercise, I allowed myself to settle into the very easy bad habit of eating shit. And then somebody thank God, called me out on it and said, 'Paul, man, you're getting fat!'

What this did was wake me up. He did me a favour because he raised the importance of me getting in shape. In order to get in shape quickly, I leveraged my fear of looking stupid by making another public declaration to my employees and my family that I was going to get back in shape, pronto! Within a month, I'd lost four kilos.

I have this thing on my desktop called a 'newsfeed eradicator'. It basically means that when I go on to Facebook, Instagram, LinkedIn, X – all those kinds of sites – this thing blocks the incoming info. Basically, there's no newsfeed, timeline or 'For You' page, so I can still use the platform, but I can't get distracted by anyone else's stuff. Procrastination is like a credit-card. A lot of fun until you get the bill!

How you live your life reveals what is truly important to you – your actions, the way you spend your time, what you surround yourself with, what you spend your money on, what you think about, what you talk about, what you read about, what you watch and what your goals are based around. That's fine when the stuff we're putting off is the stuff we don't want to do – life will always have some admin, some tedious parts, some unpleasant parts – but we have to want the end goal enough to get through the stuff we don't like on the way. But we do so often procrastinate about things that we do actually want to do – we want the end goal AND we want to do the activity. Surely, it's madness putting those things off? In fact, it's not that we don't necessarily want the things we're procrastinating over, it's either that we just want something else more, or that we're prioritising short-term goals over long-terms ones.

Most people struggle with procrastination at some point, me included. I would consider myself an action taker, but then when I'm not making progress as fast as I would like, when I am not hitting my goals in the time frame I've set, I usually blame something like lack of time or energy, when in reality, I'm probably not squeezing the most out of every single day.

I was going to call this chapter, 'How to crush procrastination' – and talk about how I – or you – would never procrastinate again. The problem is, that would indicate that procrastination is a bad thing, but that's just not correct; I've realised procrastination isn't always a bad thing. Yes, you will have to pay the bill eventually, but procrastination can be useful as it reveals your true priorities. It shows us not what we say we're going to do, but what we actually do.

Once I started to get my head around that I thought, *What if we just stop beating ourselves up for procrastinating? What if we stopped self-soothing because we're procrastinating? Maybe self-soothing and self-loathing are worse than the procrastination itself.* Rather than having to 'crush' this, 'smash' that, 'eradicate' this and 'rise' above that, I thought to myself, *How can we soften this and change the language around procrastination. How much nicer does that sound from a language point of view?* So, I'm presenting to you here the 'happy procrastination toolkit'.

What exactly is procrastination? It's putting off doing something until you can be arsed, until motivation shows up, or till you feel better; it's delaying, dithering, dilatoriness, stalling, hesitating, vacillating, dilly-dallying, and shilly-shallying. Procrastination basically means that in the moment that we're procrastinating, we're choosing to do things that give us pleasure over things that don't. I've said this before, nobody does anything to feel worse, we do everything to feel better. We talk about self-sabotage, but there's no such thing really – even when we punish ourselves, it's because we mistakenly think it will ultimately make us feel better. You took an action that at the time you thought would make you feel better and wasn't in line with who you said you would be. You took an action that in that moment made you feel better that wasn't in line with your goal. Procrastination is no different, it's choosing to do something that makes you feel better in the moment, rather than doing the thing that will make you feel worse. What if procrastination was viewed as being really helpful, because it revealed to us our most crucial priorities? How can we make taking action easier and simpler, rather than picking a fucking fight with it?

Why do we procrastinate? Fear of failure, of being rejected? How hard would it be if you agreed to do it? Is it a fear of perfectionism? Of commitment? Maybe it's that you really want to do something, but you're scared that you won't have the time to do it well, or that it'll take too much energy from something else? Are you worried it won't make you any money? Or that it will cost too much money? It might be that you just don't know what to do, so rather than find out, you just do nothing.

You hopefully know by now that I believe if you can understand the *what* and the *why*, then the *how* becomes easier. So, if you can understand *why* you procrastinate then you can question it. I get a lot of people who won't join my training programmes because they think they're going to take up too much time, yet they don't even ask me how long it's going to take. So often, the fears we hold that make us procrastinate aren't based on fact and reality. How often have you put something off only to finally do it and realise it was faster, easier and more rewarding than you thought it would be? Because we know some things are going to be difficult, we can get into the habit of imagining everything will be.

Demartini says, 'Every perception, decision and action that underlies our behaviour is an expression of our values.' In other words, if I'm not doing something it's because it's less valuable to me and lower down on my list of values. Whereas things that have high value for me – my top priorities – I am spontaneously inspired to do. But sometimes that sense of what is important can cause a glitch. I love teaching, but I'll often procrastinate when it comes to shooting training videos. What if I don't get it right? What if it doesn't go well? What if I've not got the energy? I put it off. Whereas, if I'm working on something like live training, I'm going to show up to that regardless, because I love doing that shit AND I can't let those other people down. The highest values will always be the thing that you're inspired to do. So, when you procrastinate on a task, you just need to understand that it's happening because it is lower down on your list of values. And yes, your values can change, so don't assume you will always have the same priorities.

I want to drill into values for a moment. We often think of them as beliefs – a thought or a mantra rather than something concrete. But I think values are beliefs in action. Our values are about more than what we think or say, they're shown in our choices and actions. Values are the things that you talk about AND are motivated to do. When we don't do the things that are lower down our values list, we label ourselves as lazy – but that's not the case. Labelling ourselves negatively just doesn't help. You're not lazy, you just don't know what you value.

David Goggins, the ex Navy Seal, loves pain and thrives on it. He likes running 100-mile ultra marathons because he doesn't have a problem with discipline, he loves and values it. It doesn't take discipline for me to post on social media every day, because I love and value it; it's important to me, a priority, and I'm inspired to do it. Some say, 'Oh, you need discipline to get into an ice bath.' But you don't, you're inspired to do it because it's important to you. We all have things in our lives that we're disciplined in because they're in line with our highest values. They energise us and we enjoy them, and we can see that the pay off/benefit/upside of doing them gives us more pleasure than pain.

Success leaves clues

There are areas and things in your life that you never procrastinate on, and never need to be reminded to do, nor do you need any hand-holding to do them, they just get done. I very rarely procrastinate with work-related things, specifically anything to do with teaching and coaching, as professionally, that's what I love doing the most.

Anything to do with football – whether that's watching it or training for it – I never procrastinate over. One of the first things I do when I'm free is look at where and who Sunderland are playing. I always take action. Anything to do with travel is booked months, even years in advance. Journalling is another thing that always gets done. The only reason why I never procrastinate on these things is because they tend to involve or impact other people. I would travel on my own, but I love nothing better than travelling with the family. Work involves other people and I love the social aspect. If I don't journal, I'm not my best self and that impacts my family and co-workers. For me, there's a higher perceived pleasure in coaching, travel, journalling and football than there is pain. It's not always been the case – I used to see a lot of pain in travelling because it meant taking time off work, but then I started to feel the upside in seeing the world, meeting people, getting some sun and creating magical moments.

So I'm passionate about teaching, training, travel. The word 'passion' stems from the Latin word *pati,* meaning 'to suffer'. I am willing to suffer for teaching and coaching. I am willing to put myself out there and be criticised. When I'm jujitsu training, I'm ready to get injured. I'm willing to get embarrassed and humbled. I'm willing to invest money, to lose money in business while I'm on the way to my goal. When you're really passionate about something you have to understand you will suffer for the cause. When it comes to football, I'm willing to miss out on other opportunities because of my passion for the game.

John Demartini says, 'The most growth is on the border between support and challenge, the border between pain and pleasure.' You're willing to accept both for things that are truly important to you. It's why a lot of people aren't cut out for business – because they love it when there's an upside and then they quit as soon as there is a downside. It's true for every area of life. Passion doesn't mean you only pay attention to the upsides.

Can we fix this?

Can we fix procrastination? Surely, we can't live a life only doing the things we love? It is possible to build a life where you mainly do the things that you love, but that comes largely from shifting your attitude rather than your activities. Remember, if you really love it then you are willing to take both sides of it.

You can't love something if you don't know both sides of it – that's infatuation

If I love something, it means I'm willing to take the pain and the pleasure. If I'm passionate about something it means I'm willing to suffer to get it. And loving something isn't about 'putting up' with the suffering – it's about realising that you really can't love something if you don't see it in the whole.

It's much easier to take action on something that you don't particularly want to do when it's linked to a goal, a target, an outcome. So, if you procrastinate over committing to eating well when you don't have a goal, obviously you're never going to eat well. And if that goal isn't weight loss, but the way you want to feel, you've brought the positivity back to the proposition. So when it comes to planning your actions, if you can reverse engineer it from your target and build out a plan to hit the target, then procrastination is way less likely. This is where all that goal-setting, and target-chunking we did earlier should put you in a great position – now you link it all together, and do it deliberately, not by just expecting it to happen.

'Weekly planning' is when you sit down at the start of the week and purposefully prep for the coming week; not a basic to-do list, but specific actions that you place in the calendar at a specific time, so they become a part of your schedule.

I plan out my next day the night before I leave the office, just before I go home. I like to try and keep those two worlds as separate as I can so I can give each my full attention and don't waste time in either world trying to remember what I need to do first. With my work planning, I look at what's happening tomorrow and then it's at the front of my mind the next day. On the following morning, before I fill in my journal and before I hit my six-phase meditation, I look at my calendar for a good ten to fifteen minutes thinking of the day ahead, so that when I journal it's in line with my calendar, and it's in line with my goals. And when I meditate, I know what's coming that day so I can prepare and mentally rehearse it getting done.

Ask yourself if the place where you work is conducive to taking action. I never work from home. Why? Because I procrastinate like fuck. There are loads of distractions there, and there's no sense of a deadline or of urgency. Our offices are very fast-paced and I love that. It almost becomes a competition to get shit done. Is there a good energy in your workplace? If I look forward to going into the office, then I also look forward to going home. I'm able to separate. If you aren't able to do that, then you can go and work in a coffee shop, or if your best work is done in quiet, find a library. If you like motivation, choose a smart co-working space. Find what environment away from home suits you, and your focus will grow. The reward is that when you get your work done, you get to go home and your work won't be staring you in the face there.

If you don't look forward to going in the gym, you'll procrastinate about going, sometimes until it's too late to go. So, find one that suits you. I don't particularly like lifting weights. But when I was in Abu Dhabi, I lifted three times in five days. The first day I was buzzing because Islam Makhachev, the MMA (mixed martial artist) was in the gym the day he knocked out Alexander Volkanovski. So, I trained three times whilst I was there, and yet I trained only once in Dubai, and I asked myself, *why did that happen?* I realised that I hate the gym in the Atlantis Hotel in Dubai. It's fancy as fuck with all those weird cable machines and those massage guns available for anybody that wants them. I prefer a bit more spit and sawdust, and the gym at the Abu Dhabi Hilton, while not exactly that, was just set up for people to train rather than pose and sit around. So the place where I was training made me take action. Even running with my asthma. If you look forward to going to the place where the work needs to be done, no matter what the work is, you're going to enjoy doing it more because you're energised by the environment.

I'm always productive on a flight or a train. Why? Because there's no reliable Wi-Fi: I'm distraction-free. I like to have a plan about what I'm going to do and when I'm going to do it when I take a flight. I love it. Travelling to places is never dead time for me – I arrive with the boost of knowing I've boxed off some things that I know I might have procrastinated over if I'd just left them on a list somewhere. I like delivering training, but not putting it all together. So I created a deadline, and I told my team I was going to get it done on a recent flight. I told my wife I was going to get it done. I told everybody.

Then there's people. Just being around action-takers tends to neutralise procrastination and inspires you to want to take action. How can we leverage people around us – by thinking about not just who inspires us to get stuff done, but who else is in the impact chain, who benefits from us getting things done?

Here are a few questions you can ask yourself:

1. Who benefits from this? And how do they benefit?
2. Who has already done something similar and led by example?
3. Who will I let down if it doesn't get done?
4. Who can do it with me? Who can do part of it?
5. Who can take the next steps once I've done my part?

My team benefits from it, the people I want to help will benefit from it, and my kids will benefit too, because I'll be happy, present and earning more money, which I can invest in the things they want to do. My wife will benefit from it because she's put work into it too. The sales team will benefit from it because they're going to make more cash. So when I add the *who* to the *why, what* and *how*, I add value to the task. The greater the value, the greater the chance I'll stop fucking around and just get it done.

Who can I ask for help on it?

I asked Donnie my sales guy, 'Can you take on fifty per cent of this?' It might be finding someone who can give advice on it. I might go to my business coach who'll help me ask the right questions of myself. I might choose a mentor and say, 'Mate, when you do this part which bit do you struggle with, or can you share an example of this?' We often feel bad about asking for help but remember those people we turn to get to feel like rock stars for sharing their advice or expertise.

Opportunity cost

Sometimes, even after asking for help, on some tasks you have to accept that the responsibility for it is down to you alone. And if you're going to do one thing well, that often means you're not doing something else. This is why prioritisation is key. If you've committed to doing your highest-value activity, you won't get that little inner voice bitching that you should be doing something else. But if you just pick activities at random like they're apples on a tree, you're going to be distracted by the voice in your head reminding you of all the other tasks you're not doing.

Deadlines

I love deadlines as they are one of the main procrastination predators. Some deadlines are imposed upon us and they are usually the most powerful ones because you've got that fear of letting somebody else down. But sometimes we must create our own deadlines.

If it's taking you two hours to post something on social media because you're overthinking it, don't give yourself two hours, give yourself a twenty-minute deadline. How do you do that? By putting something else in your schedule after twenty minutes. And if you don't get it done – guess what? You don't get paid.

So where can we create deadlines and urgency. I've said this before, but the reason we often avoid deadlines is because it will create stress for us. But when we procrastinate, we've already created enough stress for ourselves.

You're going to pay the bill eventually, anyway, so you may as well bring that bill forward. Urgency creates energy. Some people call it stress. I'm not going to call it that. Pressure is a privilege, and if we want to create self-imposed deadlines, we've got the privilege of being able to do that. There are many people in many areas in life who don't have the privilege of creating their own deadline.

Connect more

So you've got your *who*, *why*, *what* and *how* sorted. But if you still need some extra rocket fuel on them, you link goals in one area of your life to activity in another. Let's think of something I don't always want to do, like preparing for webinars. I love doing webinars, but I don't like putting all the content for them together first: proofreading the slides and doing the tech rehearsal. How can it fulfil what is truly important to me? But I know that not giving the best webinar I can won't just lower my energy, it won't make more sales, and if don't make more sales then I can't buy more football tickets or flights on a whim. My son and I have corporate season tickets, which means we have very expensive season tickets. I bought one for my dad as well – so we can all get access to any away game that we want. I couldn't do that unless I did things like the webinar. If I get this webinar done, then I'm going to make more sales, and if I make more sales it will enable me to travel to cooler places. If I don't do the webinar well, I'm not only losing out on opportunities to invest in more things like the tickets, I'm also devaluing the ones I've got by not getting the best use out of them. You can see now how if I take that one task, I can link it to all of the things that are important to me.

Options

Those season tickets are a great motivator for me. But what if that feels too far off? What if we need a motivator not just to start but to finish, and what if we need that motivator to be more immediate? The question now is, 'If I get this done, what's the payoff? What do I get when I finish it?'

For example, right now when I finish writing this section, I'm going to have a non-sleep deep rest. I'm going to do twenty minutes on the floor with my headphones and eye mask on. What is that? That's an incentive to get the task done and again making it more immediate. The problem with good habits is the immediate payoff is often pain. Been to the gym? Now you're aching. Finished that presentation? Now you're tired. It usually hurts, and there's usually some difficulty and no immediate pleasure. It's a longer-term benefit you're working towards. Whereas with bad habits, what do you get? Immediate gratification. The pain is longer term, so procrastination would be classed as a bad habit.

I know when I battle the urge to put things off, I need to increase the perception of pleasure and I need to make it more immediate. I found it difficult writing a book. Why?

Anything that's longer term and is delayed gratification I find difficult. I find it easy to drop a quick email. Why? Because the payoff is immediate and people respond. With a social-media post, it's immediate for me as people like it and I get a round of applause. Writing a book, though, there is no immediate payoff. So, how do I get the immediate payoff with the book that I'm working on now? I share it with my team. Maybe I make a post about it. I've got to increase the perceived pleasure and make it more immediate. You are allowed to enjoy the now as well as the future.

Exercise

1. Write down three things that you always take action on, then write down why you are always able to get these things done.
2. Questions to ask yourself to raise the value of something you're procrastinating about:

    - What is something that you're putting off currently?
    - Who will suffer if you don't do it?
    - Who gets the benefit of you doing it?
    - What are the payoffs of you doing it?
    - How can you create urgency around it?

Conclusion

What? We're at the end already? Life moves at a fair fucking gallop doesn't it! There's a Stoic term I'd like to leave you with, and this is *memento mori*, meaning 'remember that you're dying'. That's not supposed to be bleak, but it serves as a stark reminder that if you want to make the most of your life, you need to realise that it won't go on forever and that each day a little bit of it runs out. They say that the way you live out your days is the way you live your life, and if you keep putting it off till tomorrow, before you know it, it'll be too late to try and make that change.

I read this the other day and it really resonated with me: 'No one is coming. No one. No one's coming to push you, no one's coming to tell you to turn the TV off, no one's telling you to get out the door and exercise, nobody's telling you to apply for that job you've always dreamt about, nobody's coming to write that business plan for you. No one. It's up to you.'

I hope the techniques we've explored together here will help you reframe some of the ways you think and act, allowing you to better understand yourself and let your life be as electric as it can possibly be. You've got to want to change and know where you wish to go and why. But if you've got this far through the book, well, my good Mush, you've proved that you've got the minerals to Upgrade your life, and so I'd better let you get on with it.

I love the community of people I've built, and it means if you hit a bump in the road, you've got people who understand this way of thinking. Plus, I love hearing how people have found their own ways to Upgrade their lives. Do find me online and tell me what you've done.

Until we meet again, I wish you well and I believe in you.

Exercise

I couldn't resist including one last set of exercises so you leave this book inspired by the power of taking action. Hopefully, you've completed all the questions as you've gone along. But if you've been procrastinating, and left them blank, I've got you. Answer these questions now and that will put you in the right mindset for going back and filling any other blanks you've left.

1. How do you want to feel when you wake up?
2. What am I willing to do and when am I going to do it?
3. How will I make people feel today?

For free resources, tools and video masterclasses, scan the QR code below:

Acknowledgements

I'll keep this short as I'm not even sure if anyone reads it unless they're looking for their own name ;-)

First up, thanks to YOU for trusting me to guide you.

To the team at Harper North, Genevieve and Alice in particular for believing in my madness and getting my message to the masses.

To Richard Waters for unravelling and unscrambling my thoughts and philosophies over endless hours on the phone.

To my agent Luke for creating endless opportunities for me.

To the lads that gave me glowing reviews, thanks for your support.

The team at Unstoppable HQ, Cath, Connor and Sim for serving our clients and making sure I don't explode.

The Alliance and Inner Circle Squad for Inspiring me and being part of 'the cult'.

To my mam and dad for keeping me alive.

And finally to my BRILLIANT children Max and Nina for making proud on the daily. DO NOT CHANGE.

And not forgetting my incredible wife Lesley, for EVERYTHING else. Support, kindness, accountability and love. You're an inspiration and the love of my life.

Harper North

would like to thank the following staff and contributors for their involvement in making this book a reality:

Sarah Allen-Sutter
Fionnuala Barrett
Laura Braggs
Sarah Burke
Alan Cracknell
Jonathan de Peyer
Anna Derkacz
Tom Dunstan
Kate Elton
Sarah Emsley
Simon Gerratt
Lydia Grainge
Monica Green
Natassa Hadjinicolaou
Emma Hatlen
Jo Ireson
Megan Jones
Jean-Marie Kelly
Taslima Khatun
Holly Kyte
Rachel McCarron
Millie Morton
Alice Murphy-Pyle
Adam Murray
Genevieve Pegg
Amanda Percival
Laura Evans
Colleen Simpson
Eleanor Slater
Henry Steadman
Hilary Stein
Emma Sullivan
Emily Thomas
Katrina Troy
Ben Wright

For more unmissable reads,
sign up to the HarperNorth newsletter at
www.harpernorth.co.uk

or find us on socials at
@HarperNorthUK

Harper
North